To order additional copies of this book, visit your local bookstore or website and/or email: Website: https://www.emcllc.expert
Email: beyondagoodgpa@gmail.com

www.honeytreepublishingus.com

Adoo, Yaw Amponsah, 2024. Beyond a Good GPA: A Guide to Navigate Realities Never Taught in Colleges

1. College. 2. Motivational. 3. Self-Help. 4. Trade.

Cover design by Ismail Ben Design Group, Tangiers, Morocco
Interior design by Yaw Amponsah Adoo
Photographer: Nadia Yvonne Omaboe
Editor: Tytianna Ringstaff
Publisher: Honey Tree Publishing

Printed in the United States of America

Dedication

To my loving wife, Wendy Naa Kleshie Adoo, whose unwavering support made this journey possible.

To my grandparents, Edwin Amponsah Adoo and Beatrice Aku Adoo (paternal), Ludwig Koranteng Ofosu and Victoria Naa Prah Ashley (maternal): I lived to realize your dreams as a visionary leader for his people.

To my parents, Benjamin Ofosu Adoo and Amma Oduraa Adoo, and my siblings: May you always follow your curiosity and never cease to learn.

To all my mentors from kindergarten to the present, who inspired me to explore the unknown and ask the hard questions. A special thank you to the mentors of my school years at Prestea Goldfields International School, Adisadel College, and Ghana National College, who provided unwavering support and guidance. Your wisdom and encouragement have shaped my journey, and I am profoundly grateful for that.

In memory of my mentor, Dr. Jerome Gresham, who taught me the value of perseverance and hard work.

To President Kevin James of Morris Brown College, whose visionary leadership and unwavering commitment have revitalized our beloved institution. Your dedication to education, resilience, and innovation has inspired countless students, faculty, and alumni. Thank you for being a beacon of hope and a catalyst for positive change.

To all the kids in my life whom I have the privilege to mentor. Your curiosity, resilience, and boundless potential inspire me every day. This book is for you— may it encourage you to dream big, never stop learning, and always believe in yourselves.

To all the stakeholders I serve through my foundation, The Adoo Family Foundation. Your trust, collaboration, and unwavering support fuel our mission and drive our success. This book is a testament to our shared vision and commitment to positively impacting our communities. Thank you for being an integral part of this journey.

For those who dare to dream and strive for knowledge, this book is dedicated to you.

Acknowledgment

I am grateful to my publisher and editor, Dr. Tytianna Ringstaff, for her meticulous attention to detail and for helping to bring my vision to life.

Table of Contents

Foreward

In today's competitive world, achieving a good GPA is often seen as the golden ticket to success. Yet, as many recent graduates soon discover, there's much more to thriving professionally than stellar academic performance. *Beyond A Good GPA* is an enlightening guide that takes you on a transformative journey beyond the confines of grades and transcripts into real-world skills, resilience, and continuous personal development.

As a recent graduate, you stand at the precipice of exciting yet uncharted territory. The transition from academia to the professional world can be daunting, filled with uncertainties and challenges that a high GPA alone cannot navigate. The book is crafted precisely for you—to equip you with the insights, tools, and perspectives necessary to survive, excel, and find fulfillment in your career and beyond.

The crux of the book is the idea that success is multifaceted. While your academic achievements are commendable, they are just one piece of the puzzle. The book delves into the essential soft skills critical for career advancement: communication, emotional intelligence, adaptability, and leadership. Through compelling anecdotes and practical advice, you'll learn how to harness these skills to distinguish yourself in any professional setting.

In a rapidly changing world, adapting, persevering, and exercising resilience is invaluable. The book offers strategies for developing a resilient mindset, teaching you how to turn setbacks into opportunities for growth and maintain a positive outlook in the face of adversity. Resilience, one of the most striking segments of the book, is particularly resonant for recent graduates who may be encountering the first significant hurdles of their careers.

Success in the professional world is as much about who you know as what you know. The book thoroughly explores networking—how to build meaningful connections, the art of effective communication, and the importance of mentorship. By leveraging these relationships, you can open doors to opportunities that might otherwise remain closed.

Lifelong learning is also emphasized. The knowledge acquired in college is just the beginning. This book encourages a mindset of continuous education—whether through further formal studies, professional development courses, or self-directed learning. This dedication to personal growth will keep you agile and competitive in your career.

Throughout the book, you will find inspiring stories from successful individuals who have navigated the path you are about to embark on. Their journeys illustrate that while a good GPA can open doors, the additional qualities and experiences sustain long-term success. These narratives are powerful reminders that your potential is limitless when you embrace a holistic personal and professional development approach.

The book is more than a guide; it's a companion for your journey from college graduate to accomplished professional. It empowers you to look beyond your academic achievements and equips you with the necessary skills to thrive in the real world. As you turn these pages, be prepared to challenge yourself, grow, and redefine what success means to you.

Welcome to the beginning of an exciting new chapter. Your future is beyond a good GPA—it's filled with boundless potential and endless possibilities. Embrace it with confidence and curiosity.

Dr. Nasrolah R. Farokhi
𝔓𝔯𝔬𝔣𝔢𝔰𝔰𝔬𝔯 𝔈𝔪𝔢𝔯𝔦𝔱𝔲𝔰
Morris Brown College

This foreword is graciously provided by Dr. Nasrolah Farokhi, a distinguished figure whose career spans 43 years of remarkable achievements in both academia and humanitarian efforts. Dr. Farokhi's dedication to education and human welfare has earned him numerous regional and international awards. His unparalleled commitment to fostering knowledge and compassion has left an indelible mark on countless lives, making him a beacon of inspiration for generations to come. His words in this foreword continue his legacy of empowering others to reach their fullest potential, setting the stage for the invaluable insights contained in this book.

Preface

In reality, college only teaches you some of what you need for a successful career. As a result, this book is designed to guide and help you leverage the degree you've earned. Whether you're a high school senior, college freshman, traditional or non-traditional student, first-generation college student, international student, a recent graduate, or on the brink of entering the workforce, it is your choice to make the most of your college degree and enact the change you seek by navigating the path to success beyond college.

As an international college student who faced the stressors of navigating undergraduate college life while competing and thriving alongside American peers, completing final exams, and realizing the significance of seizing every opportunity, I am here to offer my personal experiences, valuable insights, practical advice, and creative strategies to empower students to overcome obstacles and achieve their academic and professional goals. With this book as your companion, tips on securing a job, excelling in your career, and making a difference in the world are offered. The goal is to help equip you to make the most of your college education and degree, take on whatever challenges come your way, and build a prosperous future for yourself, turning your dreams into reality.

Many of us have faced various challenges throughout life, especially during college, with financial struggles being the most common (i.e., increasing tuition rates, textbooks, and living expenses). Balancing work and academics are obstacles, especially for those who must work to support themselves and their families. Additionally, inadequate academic preparation in high school or limited access to resources can make it difficult for some students to keep up with their coursework. Further compounding these challenges, mental health issues, such as stress, anxiety, and depression, affect academic performance and overall well-being.

Despite these barriers, learners deserve opportunities to excel, which is why this book is designed for those who need support while in the game to succeed in becoming the captain of our ship. This book addresses the challenges many face beyond the classroom, from taking exams to landing internships.

As the architect of your destiny, transitioning into the professional world, your abilities and skills, such as social and emotional learning, collaborative team building, time management, and intentional communication through tone, candor, respectability, and tactfulness, are paramount to your role in the workforce. We must operate in our abilities and skills, ensuring we stand out from the crowd as visionary leaders, taking ownership of our lives, goals, and dreams. And, if you need more skills, don't despair. Remember that every person is trainable, and plenty of resources are available to help you.

You must understand that your presence in a company has nothing to do with your good grades or your previous successful work in college or with a former employer. In this book, you will learn teachable skill sets to best navigate the nuances of the workforce during your life after college journey. Along this path, it is essential to aim higher than academic expectations. Entering the workforce, you are expected to apply the same determination and perseverance nurtured as a college student in your new journey as a career professional. The goal is to unlock your full potential and achieve greatness in every aspect of your life. Thriving in the work environment requires you to market and sell your skills effectively.

Discussed broadly by many guests on my podcast, *The Ability Project*, tips are shared during the *What Employers Want* series on how to market yourself during a job interview. This podcast series – streamed across over 50 countries on Spotify and Apple – is the reason for this book. The inspirational stories shared throughout this series of ordinary individuals who have overcome obstacles are models of success.

Just as this podcast has equipped listeners and readers with the knowledge and motivation to pursue their dreams relentlessly, this book is also a resource for individuals who have been historically overlooked and disregarded from having equivalent educational advantages or opportunities as others. This book is also a testament to the resilience and determination of those who refuse to be defined by their circumstances. Serving as a beacon of hope for anyone facing challenges or setbacks, this book acknowledges that success is possible with perseverance and sustained with a positive mindset.

Within these pages, I hope the practical guidance through real-life stories and actionable tips inspire you to push through adversity and achieve your goals. I also hope this book guides and triggers your curiosity to learn more about you and helps you discover the necessary tools to build your path, chase after your aspirations, and take control of your destiny while forging and treading a unique path. No matter your journey, know that you can shape your future and steer your life in the desired direction.

By sharing my story, my mission is to help challenge you to think critically and creatively beyond your diploma about your contribution to the professional world. Together, let's break through the barriers holding us back and forge our paths to success, harnessing the power of education and ambition to create a brighter future for ourselves and those who come after us. Join me on this journey of exploration and empowerment as we uncover the keys to success together.

EDUCATOR | MANAGEMENT CONSULTANT

CHAPTER 1

Welcome to REAL Life!

"That strong mother doesn't tell her cub, Son, stay weak so the wolves can get you. She says, 'Toughen up, this is reality we are living in'" (Lauryn Hill Quotes, n.d.).

Lauryn Hill

Lauryn Hill is a member of Fugees from the critically acclaimed solo album, *The Miseducation of Lauryn Hill.*

CONGRATULATIONS! You made it through four arduous years of noteworthy studying, partying, home visits, more studying, retaking courses, more intense studying, completing internships (maybe), and studying for the final course of your academic experience. You may have studied abroad, volunteered, joined campus clubs and student organizations, held jobs, made the dean's list, pulled an all-nighter, had a roommate, got into a relationship, played college-level sports, participated in college events, and possibly took a road trip with your craziest friends.

You may feel excitement and apprehension as you stand on the brink of adulthood with the tassel of your graduation cap dangling by your side. Perhaps the journey has been a whirlwind of tests, essays, friendships, and memories. But now, as you prepare to step into the REAL world, ponder on the words of the nurturing mother: "… tough love as the guiding light." (Lauryn Hill Quotes, n.d.). Gone are the days of sheltered hallways and regimented, scheduled classes in high school, where the yellow school bus was guaranteed to pick you up and drop you off safely home. The time is near to face the wolves head-on, armed with knowledge from textbooks and resilience and determination instilled by those who have guided you.

Welcome to the REAL life − where challenges await you and purposeful opportunities for growth and triumph. You see, the degree you have earned is possibly *the* most vital tool to use for REAL life. Like a passport and a visa, the diploma is just a means to your end. Some of your peers think the outcomes of the diploma solve all of life's problems, primarily when you have worked hard to earn those extraordinary GPAs, accolades, and the like. However, this couldn't be farther from the truth. What is true is that the road to the diploma was an opportunity to develop mental toughness further. The reality is that when you are faced with tough situations, only training can bail you out.

Looking back over my life, I find it intriguing how my grades in college, As and Bs, were unrelated to the real-life challenges I now face. Only a few professors took the time to practically show students like me what to expect in my career and how best to use my earned skills. As an educator, I have learned that many college professors, tutors, and mentors also received little guidance as college students. This is a major issue in the educational sector. In a way, I couldn't blame them for not providing the advice that all students needed when they hadn't acquired it themselves during their college years.

I was humbled to attend and complete college within seven years, during which time I earned my bachelor's and master's degrees from East Stroudsburg University in the Commonwealth of Pennsylvania—as an international student from Ghana – a nation on West Africa's Gulf of Guinea known for diverse wildlife, old forts, secluded beaches, and now oil and lithium – the weight of academic expectations to achieve at the highest level as the eldest son in my community, and especially as a male, posed unique challenges.

As a child, I never enjoyed my boyhood and early adulthood. As I reflect on my childhood, I can't help but feel a deep sense of empathy for the young person I once was. As the oldest of many siblings, I often felt incredibly lonely without older brothers or sisters to guide me. While my younger sister seemed to have all the fun, I struggled to navigate the world independently.

That loneliness only intensified when my parents traveled to Europe for school, leaving me in the care of my grandparents. During that time, I felt like such a peculiar and fragile child, without many close friends to whom I could turn. The few friendships I did manage to cultivate, I cherished deeply. Yet, no matter how hard I tried, I never felt like I truly belonged.

Looking back, I wish I could reach out to that young, isolated version of myself and let them know that the loneliness and sense of not fitting in wouldn't last forever. That one day, I would find my tribe, my people, the ones who would truly see and understand me. But in those formative years, when craving guidance and a sense of belonging, I was left to fend for myself, doing my best to navigate the complexities of growing up.

Experiences like these have shaped me into the person I am today. The resilience I developed, the empathy I gained, and the determination to never let another young person feel as alone as I once did are the gifts that emerged from my struggles. And now, as I look ahead to the next chapter of my life, I'm driven to pay it forward, to be the mentor and guiding light that I so desperately needed back then.

Some children at school didn't want to hang out with me because they thought I was strange, while others wanted to hang out with me only if I gave them something, like sharing my soccer ball (or sandwich, LOL). However, I craved attention, played independently, and dreamed of a future without many responsibilities. Furthermore, I dreamed about what I wanted to be when I grew up – an astronaut, architect, painter, or artist. My paternal grandpa even wanted me to be a priest. But I ended up becoming a teacher instead. When I was 12, I realized education was the key to achieving my dreams. That's when everything changed for me.

My parents didn't know their advice to excel was moot, as I already was self-motivated. Growing up, my mom, who provided more emotional support, would tell me, *"Learn for me, okay? When you learn, no one can take it away from you."* On the other hand, my dad would often say, in his deep voice, *"Yaw, you can drive the Carina II after you pass the O'-levels."* He always pushed me to pursue a STEM career (Science, Technology, Engineering, and Mathematics) like him, even when I was young. I did everything I could to resist that path as a way of rebelling against my dad's strict approach to parenting. Looking back over my childhood, I wish my dad could have been more laid-back and interacted with me differently. Now that I'm an adult, I understand that many African parents, especially fathers, were raised differently. However, I have made peace with my father's strict parenting style and found the right mindset that does not affect my mental well-being.

As a kid, I didn't feel like I fit in much. I was the oldest, without older siblings to show me the ropes. My baby sister, our youngest, was two years younger and seemed to have all the fun. I craved attention and dreamed of a future where I wouldn't have so many responsibilities. When my parents went to Europe for school, I stayed with my grandparents and felt lonely. I struggled with talking to people and making friends. While I had a few friends, some kids thought I was strange and only wanted to hang out with me if I gave them something, like sharing my soccer ball.

Reality set in quickly when I turned 12. At that age, I understood that hitting the books was the key to a bright future. This meant I had to read more and learn as much as possible about everything around me. The problem was that I could have been better at taking tests. I struggled to prepare adequately, especially for my G.C.E Ordinary and Advanced-level exams. The dread and fear of hearing the words, "*Get ready to stop work!*" by the exam supervisors weighed heavily on me. It wasn't that I didn't know the material; I did. The intent to take an exam was to pass, not to fail, but the tone of those words led to a feeling of overwhelming doom. To this day, I still don't understand why they said those words.

The excitement of learning alone was fun for me. I enjoyed the process of grinding for perfection. I loved striving for perfection. In primary school, I once earned an award for being the top student in a subject. Then, at Adisadel College – my high school – I was usually somewhere in the middle of the pack. Adisadel College was and is still considered one of the best schools in Africa, consistently ranking in the top 10 across various categories. Even in subjects where I didn't perform as well on exams, I studied all the material so I could know more than my classmates.

My experience navigating campus life in the Poconos at East Stroudsburg unfolded in stages. Before 1997, I had never experienced air travel. My only prior taste of international travel was a family road trip to Elubo Beach, a town in the western region of Ghana, near the border of the Ivory Coast (the Republic of Côte d'Ivoire). This coastal country boasts beach resorts, lush rainforests, and a rich French colonial heritage. Packed into a VW Beetle, all seven of us embarked on this memorable journey with my parents up front. I can still recall the feeling of the wind streaming through the rolled-down windows and how I cherished those breezy moments as I daydreamed. At Elubo, I vividly remember the scare when my youngest sibling briefly went missing on the beach and the frantic search to find her. Thanks to her curious nature, the relief of locating my sister Korantemaa was palpable.

I always knew I would travel abroad one day, but I never anticipated the extent to which it would happen. I understood that my opportunity for international travel would come solely through academic endeavors. My father, whom I deeply admire and am incredibly grateful for, always had a vision for our family. He recognized that my success as the eldest would set the stage for my siblings to thrive. My father was prepared when the chance finally arose after several missed opportunities. He invested all his savings to send me abroad – purchasing a ticket, covering one semester's tuition, and providing pocket money.

The family trip to Elubo Beach and my journey to the United States of America, particularly New York, in the fall of 1997 were vastly different experiences — the former provided security, support, and the close bond of family without direct responsibility. The latter placed all the weight on my shoulders. I had no room for academic failure. Every exam served as a reminder of the pressure to succeed. I couldn't afford to lose sight of my purpose. It felt like a make-or-break situation. For a long time, I used the total cost of my airfare to John F. Kennedy International Airport (JFK) as the password for many of my sensitive accounts. That's how intertwined my life became with my journey to the U.S.

In 1997, I landed at JFK Airport to start college, a year filled with significant events. Back then, Ghana had only one national airline, Ghana Airways. It was the airline my father could afford for my journey to East Stroudsburg University, and New York was its sole destination. It was the year of Hong Kong's independence from China, the cloning of Dolly the sheep, the tragic mass suicide of members of the Heaven's Gate cult in San Diego, California, O. J. Simpson's loss in his civil suit for wrongful death, Timothy McVeigh's conviction for the Oklahoma City bombing, the successful landing of the Mars Pathfinder on Mars, and the world bidding farewell to Princess Diana.

As I watched these events unfold on cable news, I felt overwhelmed. I struggled to process these significant world events without easy access to the internet like today. The mass suicide left me confused, O.J. Simpson's case highlighted racial divides, and Princess Diana's death left me with a sense of deep sadness.

In a new country, I had to adapt to everything new. I arrived in January and had to deal with the bitter, wintry, cold weather. Before arriving in the U.S., I thought I could handle the weather. To prepare, I had intentionally stuck my hand for many minutes in a freezer in my home in Accra, Ghana's capital, similar in size (15.9 cubic feet) to a Galaxy CF16 commercial chest freezer. I thought, *I got this*. However, the 27°F weather crushed my feelings and rocked me cold to the bone. Dr. Samuel Quainoo and Dr. Tina Q. Richardson – accomplished academics – became like family to me. They were there to welcome me when I arrived at JFK Airport to begin my academic journey. I recall feeling hesitant to step outside because of the cold, but they were prepared with warm clothing to ensure my comfort during my stay.

Preparing for the undergraduate academic workload and extra-curricular activities required more than mental, psychological, and physical presence. And to top it off, I was dealing with homesickness to no avail. Might I add, dealing with homesickness is tougher than acing a class with a solid A. I quickly learned that international student departments on many campuses unfortunately don't have the core elements to communicate this misery, which makes it nearly impossible for many American students to understand the torture. The reality is that many American college campuses often need to catch up and be equipped to guide and provide adequate support, which leads to student success, especially for international students.

This sentiment was echoed by many international students at East Stroudsburg University and across campuses during my college years. The challenges international students face, from homesickness to navigating holidays on campus (or with host families), missing familiar food and cultural events, language barriers, discrimination, inability to work off-campus, concerns about scholarship loss, and missing loved ones, are often overlooked.

It always felt like everything was twice as difficult to achieve. Across campuses, while staff at International

Student Affairs have good intentions, they usually need more cultural understanding of the unique challenges international students encounter.

To navigate this reality, many international students instinctively bond – regardless of which part of the world they come from – to work together in many ways to survive on campuses. Lessons from community-building helped us as we grew up, pursued careers, and built networks. This strong bond enables us to support each other in the U.S. and abroad. Through shared experiences, we've learned to rely on one another for advice, encouragement, and practical assistance, creating a network far beyond campus borders. This solidarity has helped us navigate the challenges of college life and served us well as we transition into the professional world.

Upon graduation, graduates must focus on many vital aspects to set them up for success in life. It is no secret that the priorities are scary, demanding, and stimulating, all at the same time. As you navigate your college journey and explore your future, regardless of where you currently stand in your academic path, here are some tips to help you:

Visualize your Future. Again, the degree is a means to your vision. It would be best if you found a clear roadmap. Your degree will get you to where you need to be. Say your vision is to become a college professor. You must prepare to pursue a master's and/or doctorate in a field you intend to teach. You must understand and become comfortable with this profession's privilege, politics, socioeconomic, legal, technological, and cultural implications. From my experience in academia, I see that many professors have a communal mandate to change their communities through their profession. They shape their communities through instruction, applied research, scholarly activity, and service that support the institutional mission to foster collegial relationships with supervisors, peers, students, and the college community.

Seek Professional Mentors. Choose professors whose careers you idolize and learn from them. Access mentors and sponsors for advice on visualizing your future, as shared by Carla Harris (2014). Mentors are not the same as sponsors. Mentors are experienced and trusted advisors. We all have mentors. In contrast, a sponsor is someone who's *"got your back"* professionally and will speak for you at the decision-making table for your desired opportunities. This may be the right time to select mentors and sponsors from many disciplines to guide you. Be sure to choose those who will tell you the hard truths about what you need to hear. Seek mentors from all traditional and non-traditional avenues, including, but not limited to, spiritual counselors to financial professionals, as well as social media pathways. Either way, ensure you update them on your professional quests. Getting in touch with them every quarter of the year is not a bad habit. Share your professional struggles, disappointments, and conflicts with them. More importantly, they always have questions available for them to answer. Take their advice seriously, assuring them you intend to consider their input.

Focus on Passion, not Money. Your vision must *never* be about money first. It must instead be about passion. Focusing solely on money may disrupt your consciousness in the long run. Remember that with a college degree, the likelihood of you becoming financially secure is higher than people without college degrees. Many graduates with little experience may be convinced that money is everything. Not so true. While money makes living very convenient, assures self-confidence, and possibly saves lives, it may lead to unnecessary chaos if you are still determining your visualized future.

Define Your Professional Goals. Have a clear idea of what you want to accomplish professionally. Do you want to build a school? Operate a non-profit organization? Establish a consultancy firm? Whatever you want to achieve, use course objectives and competencies from some of the critical classes you took in college. This information is often found in the course curriculum and/or syllabus, which can guide you in aligning your educational experiences with your career goals.

Join Professional Organizations. Joining professional organizations is also crucial for gaining first-hand information about your chosen profession. These memberships are generally more affordable for new graduates compared to what seasoned professionals pay. Additionally, the benefits of being a member can significantly expedite your career transition. You'll have the opportunity to connect with like-minded professionals who are often willing and able to support your journey, providing valuable networking and mentorship opportunities.

Faith and Wisdom for Career Success. If you are a person of faith, be more in tune with your deity for greater wisdom and strength for endurance. You will need it. Prayers and meditation help a lot but understand that much of the work is solely up to you to accomplish. Seek wisdom from those who have been through what you are about to go through. Pray that you instinctively find the right person at the right time for what you need. Be bold and ask questions. It's essential not to stay quiet about what you need. For those who are shy, this is the best time to learn to become an extrovert for your future career. No one will care more for your career than you do. You can start a social group with like-minded recent graduates to encourage each other with positive information regarding your careers and futures.

CHAPTER 2

What my boss needs is...

"When I was born, some of our relatives came to our house and told my mother, 'Don't worry, next time you will have a son'" (Malala Yousafzai Quotes, n.d.).

Malala Yousafzai

Malala Yousafzai is a Pakistani activist for female education and the youngest-ever Nobel Prize laureate.

This chapter explores what it truly means to be valued and respected in the workplace and how to navigate and challenge the biases that may stand in your way. In addition to practical advice, the chapter will include relevant technical language to help illustrate the importance of these concepts in a professional setting. So, what does your boss need from you? Let's find out together, while also breaking down the technicalities that will help you better understand and navigate the workplace.

A cultural expectation of academic excellence seemed to add to the pressure to succeed. Navigating this pressure was daunting, especially considering the limited resources and support available. Yet, failure was not an option. I was determined to achieve academic success not just for myself but for my family and community.

While many students excel at studying and achieving high grades, more is needed to guarantee success beyond the classroom. While a college student, I had to develop strategies to retain and apply the knowledge acquired despite not being a good test taker. This was emotionally draining for me.

The frustration of graduating and facing uncertainty post-graduation, unsure of how to navigate the job market, is a shared experience. It's essential to recognize that success requires more than just academic prowess. Success demands understanding the nuances and skills only sometimes taught in traditional teaching and learning spaces.

Employers seek candidates who are not only academically qualified but also equipped with practical skills and real-world experience. It can be even more challenging to seize professional opportunities like internships and excel academically. It reminds us that earning a degree is just the start; we must actively promote ourselves and demonstrate our skills during interviews to land the desired opportunities.

As college students, we must seize every opportunity to gain hands-on experience and prove our value in the workforce. That means taking full advantage of internships, externships, and other opportunities offering work-ready experiences.

Bias is deep-seated in our culture. As you step into the work world, you may carry the weight of societal expectations and stereotypes. The expectations often revolve around inequity around traditional gender roles, racial biases, and socioeconomic status. Remember that your worth is not determined by the societal biases placed upon you. Depending on the society, women may be expected to prioritize family over career, minorities to conform to certain cultural norms, and those from lower-income backgrounds to struggle to succeed.

Stereotypes about intelligence, work ethic, and capabilities based on factors like race, gender, or background can also hinder one's professional growth. These stereotypes and expectations can create added pressure and barriers to success in the workplace, requiring individuals to navigate them skillfully while striving to achieve their goals. Despite these challenges, it's essential to remain focused, resilient, and determined to defy these expectations and prove one's worth.

How do you like them future "apples"? In other words, how does the future of your career look? There are many skills employers and industries expect from college graduates. In the job market, employers and industries seek many skills in new hires, with communication and problem-solving being the two most prominent.

First, employers highly prize communication skills across various sectors. Effective communication is essential for conveying ideas, collaborating with colleagues, and interacting with clients or customers. Whether verbal communication in meetings, written communication in emails and reports, or nonverbal communication through body language, the ability to express oneself clearly and articulately is crucial. For graduating seniors like you, Kevin Gray reported in the National Association of Colleges and Employers (NACE), citing the 2023 Student Survey, that communication, critical thinking, and teamwork were listed as the top competencies for career readiness (Gray, 2024). Similarly, employers in NACE's Job Outlook 2024 survey emphasized these three skills as crucial for job candidates.

Figure 2: Student and employer ratings of student proficiency in career readiness competencies, by percent of respondents

Competency	New Graduates	Employers
Communication	79.4%	55.2%
Critical Thinking	81.5%	66.1%
Teamwork	86.9%	78.1%
Career & Self-Development	63.9%	47.1%
Professionalism	84.6%	50.0%
Leadership	68.5%	36.8%
Technology	68.1%	81.7%
Equity & Inclusion	81.0%	70.8%

NACE.
National Association of
Colleges and Employers

Source: National Association of Colleges and Employers. Data are from NACE's *2023 Student Survey* and *Job Outlook 2024 Survey*. These are the percentages of responding students and employers that, on a five-point scale, rated recent graduates either "very proficient" (4) or "extremely proficient" (5) in the respective competency.

Second, problem-solving skills are in high demand in today's dynamic work environment. Employers value individuals who think critically, analyze situations, and devise innovative solutions to complex problems. Whether it's troubleshooting technical issues, resolving conflicts among team members, or identifying inefficiencies in processes, the ability to approach challenges with a problem-solving mindset is essential. According to a survey by the Association of American Colleges and Universities (AAC&U), 93% of employers consider critical thinking and problem-solving skills more important than a candidate's undergraduate major.

Employers prefer to hire graduates experienced in many professional aspects beyond their degrees. For example, college graduates in the STEM field do not often face this issue as their coursework prepares them to enter the STEM industries, according to Ashley Finley, AAC&U Vice President for Research for AAC&U

(Finley, 2021). As a result, STEM students are considered the most sought-after candidates due to their employable skills, presenting them with numerous employment opportunities, unlike college graduates in other fields of study. While all disciplines should prepare college students to enter the workforce, this is not the case, leading to a significant issue in higher education. Many students are taught to prioritize excellent grades rather than applying content and skills learned in their academic pathway to fulfill employer and industry needs (Finley, 2023). Employers desire college graduates who demonstrate the following traits:

1. Utilizing critical thinking and problem-solving skills which means finding efficient ways to analyze problems by breaking them down into smaller parts.
2. Applying current industry standards correctly to demonstrate both technical competence and a commitment to maintaining the quality and integrity of their work, ensuring they are

valuable and reliable assets to the organization. This ability is crucial because it shows that the graduate is up-to-date with industry practices, which is essential for achieving organizational goals and maintaining competitive advantage.

3. Working effectively in diverse teams, such as being culturally aware and recognizing biases like cognitive bias.

4. Using relevant information to produce high-quality work, showing logical reasoning and the ability to predict performance standards.

5. Sharing knowledge and skills, lessons from leaders, and passing that knowledge on to others, especially in team settings.

6. Communicating effectively, both verbally and in writing, with strong interpersonal skills and convincing written and digital communications

7. Collaborating effectively with others is crucial. Even when finding group work challenging, employers like it when employees work well

with others, share tasks, and help the team succeed.

8. Embodying digital skills is essential, too. It might be tricky, but using technology to enhance work skills is something employers expect as technology continues to improve.

9. Promoting teamwork and collaboration skills developed through group assignments. While some students find group work challenging, graduates with strong social and emotional intelligence who can actively participate, share responsibilities, and contribute meaningfully to team success are highly valued by employers.

If you have ever felt uneasy around technology, I understand your concerns. Before I arrived in Pennsylvania many moons ago, the closest I had come to touching a computer was one nicely laid out on the October 24, 1988, *Newsweek* magazine cover entitled; *"Mr. Chips: Steve Jobs Puts the 'Wow' Back in Computers"* (Newsweek, 1988). It felt scary to think about operating that machine. However, with grit and perseverance, I became a tutor in my second semester on campus for the COMP 101 course for many students who needed help. The takeaway is that you can overcome your fear of computers or anything (for that matter) with the proper support.

Employers expect graduates to combine knowledge, skills, and attitudes using technology to perform tasks, solve problems, communicate and manage information, and collaborate to create and share digital content that is appropriate, creative, critical, ethical, independent, and secure.

Employers seek graduates who possess strong leadership skills. The article *"The Most Important Leadership Competencies, According to Leaders Around the World"* was published in *Harvard Business Review* in 2016 by Dr. Sunnie Giles, renowned for her expertise in

The Top 10 Leadership Competencies, Grouped Into Five Themes

When 195 global leaders were asked to rate 74 qualities, these rose to the top.

PERCENTAGE OF RESPONDENTS

Theme	%	Competency
Strong ethics & safety	67%	Has high ethical and moral standards
Self-organizing	59	Provides goals and objectives with loose guidelines/direction
	56	Clearly communicates expectations
Efficient learning	52	Has the flexibility to change opinions
Nurtures growth	43	Is committed to my ongoing training
Connection & belonging	42	Communicates often and openly
	39	Is open to new ideas and approaches
	38	Creates a feeling of succeeding and failing together
	38	Helps me grow into a next-generation leader
	37	Provides safety for trial and error

SOURCE SUNNIE GILES   © HBR.ORG

Source: Giles (2016).

radical innovation, and stands among numerous respected authorities in leadership. In her research, Dr. Giles conducted interviews with 195 global leaders from 15 countries, including China, Germany, India, Japan, the United Kingdom, and the U.S., to identify the top 10 out of 74 leadership competencies (Giles, 2016).

Leading with integrity and prioritizing safety were identified as the most crucial traits. Graduate students are advised to refine their ability to set a positive example for others using Dr. Giles' criteria. This involves striving to be a role model to benefit others.

To achieve this, graduates must establish honesty, respect, fairness, and community-building standards. When it comes to self-organizing tasks, graduates should adopt the practice of giving "loose guidelines and direction" instead of strict directives. This approach empowers highly skilled team members by offering recommendations rather than imposing rigid instructions, fostering a more collaborative and adaptive work environment.

Employers expect graduates to exhibit professionalism and a strong work ethic. Graduates must demonstrate a strong work ethic and personal accountability, like showing up early, managing time wisely, and working efficiently with a team.

New graduates must show honesty and moral integrity while being determined to succeed, recognizing that success can mean different things to different people, especially in America. In a world of challenges and temptations, integrity is a cornerstone of character. It means being truthful and transparent in all our actions and decisions. It also involves treating others respectfully and fairly, regardless of their background or beliefs.

Being honest and morally upright builds trust and credibility for success in any endeavor, including the workplace. Being held accountable for one's actions is an attribute reserved for the best and brightest. Accountability for actions is an expectation of the most capable individuals. These individuals are academically successful and firm in their moral character and integrity as role models, trusted to lead by example in various aspects of life.

New graduates must express a willingness to work hard. Success doesn't just happen overnight. It requires dedication and effort. By putting in the hours and striving for excellence, goals are achievable. Hard work also demonstrates our commitment and determination to succeed, setting us apart from those who are content with mediocrity. It's about going the extra mile and pushing ourselves beyond our limits to reach new heights, as the rewards of our hard work are well worth the effort.

For some, success is measured by financial wealth and career advancement; for others, it's about personal fulfillment and positively impacting society. In America, success is often associated with achieving the *American Dream*, which includes owning a home, starting a family, and having a successful career. However, success can also be defined by personal goals and aspirations, such as pursuing one's passion or making a difference in the world (Taussig, 2021). Ultimately, success is a journey, and it's up to everyone to define what it means to them and work tirelessly to achieve it.

New graduates must also be adaptable. Flexibility is required to handle situations such as different challenges that may come our way. Sometimes, we might find ourselves in complicated situations, but it's essential to keep pushing forward. Adapting to these situations can help us grow and develop personally and professionally. When you learn from your experiences, you become stronger.

Employers seek new hires who consistently deliver results. Getting the job done translates to being dependable and responsible. Employers are looking for graduates who complete tasks and do so efficiently and effectively. It's not just about finishing the job; it's about doing it well and meeting or exceeding expectations. This means producing high-quality work that demonstrates skills and capabilities.

Employers value professionals who deliver results consistently and on time, showing that we can be relied upon to complete tasks. Our ability to perform at a high level and achieve tangible outcomes sets us apart and makes us valuable assets to employers.

Emotional intelligence is the awareness of and managing our own emotions while also understanding and empathizing with the feelings of others. This skill helps build strong relationships with coworkers, clients, and supervisors, which can lead to greater job satisfaction and success. Employers value graduates with emotional intelligence because it helps create a positive work environment and fosters effective communication and collaboration among team members.

Employers recognize that graduates with high emotional intelligence are better equipped to handle workplace challenges and conflicts, resulting in improved productivity and teamwork. Developing emotional intelligence enhances professional growth and contributes to the organization's success.

Many employers expect graduates to develop emotional intelligence with little cost to the organizational budget. Rather than requiring expensive investments, these programs focus on personal growth and development, benefiting both individuals and organizations. Participating in such training can improve our ability to handle workplace challenges and cultivate positive relationships with colleagues. These skills, including self-awareness, empathy, and effective communication, can be developed through targeted training initiatives without requiring significant financial resources. Emotional intelligence training can lead to a more harmonious and productive work environment while minimizing costs for the organization, making it a valuable and cost-effective investment in the professional development of employees.

In college, we often repeat the same classroom routines and exercises that may not prepare us for the nuanced challenges of the real professional world. While repetition can help us become proficient in specific skills, repeating tasks over and over doesn't necessarily translate to thinking critically or solving complex problems.

Employers value individuals who can adapt to new situations and think creatively, skills that are only sometimes honed through repetitive exercises. Instead of focusing solely on repetition, we should seek opportunities to engage in activities that require us to apply our knowledge in novel ways and think outside the box. By doing so, we can better prepare ourselves for the dynamic and ever-changing demands of the professional world.

Possessing a positive attitude suggests a willingness to embrace inconveniences. A self-motivated graduate is self-regulated to keep their "eyes on the ball." A positive attitude means being open to challenges and inconveniences with optimism and determination. Maintaining a positive mindset allows us to persevere and focus on our goals when encountering setbacks or obstacles.

A self-motivated graduate takes the initiative and proactively pursues their objectives, even when faced with difficulties or setbacks. They possess the self-discipline to stay on track and prioritize tasks effectively, ensuring they remain focused and productive. By embracing inconveniences and maintaining a positive attitude, self-motivated graduates demonstrate their resilience and determination to succeed, setting themselves apart as valuable assets in the professional world.

Employers value graduates with career management skills, which involve various strategies for planning, developing, and advancing one's career. Career management encompasses setting clear career goals, identifying opportunities for growth and advancement, and actively seeking professional development opportunities.

It also involves effective communication and networking skills to build relationships with peers, mentors, and industry professionals. Additionally, career management includes the ability to adapt to changes in the job market and industry trends and the capacity to make informed decisions about career paths and opportunities. Overall, mastering career management helps with navigating the complexities of the job market and achieving long-term career success.

Employers understand that new graduates may need to gain experience in their new careers. As a result, they may prefer experienced candidates to fill open positions. However, this should not discourage new graduates. Instead, graduates are encouraged to engage in non-paid career-related internship activities at any given time to boost their search for positions in their desired careers. They can accomplish this by doing three things:

(1) getting better at communicating and working well with others,

(2) using career information to keep learning throughout life, and

(3) making intelligent choices about lifelong learning.

There are many ways to sharpen interaction skills. One way is regulatory. For example, the 2020 global pandemic forced the workplace environment to adapt to unique interactions between and among employees and other stakeholders with safety in mind (Kaushik & Guleria, 2020). During that time, federal agencies mandated face masks and social distancing of at least six feet. State and local governments also enforce these rules, as do many private businesses. Another example of people's interaction skills is recognizing how career choices affect work-life balance. For instance, imagine you are a new graduate taking on a demanding work project to gain experience and showcase your abilities. As you invest more time and effort into this project, you might need to sharpen your interaction skills to manage professional commitments and personal responsibilities. Loved ones relying on you, like a family member who needs care or a partner who depends on your emotional support, create an ongoing learning experience. Balancing these responsibilities requires effective communication, empathy, and time management. This experience not only strengthens your interaction skills but also prepares you for seeking additional training or projects in your field. By navigating these challenges, you can achieve a better work-life balance while continuing to grow professionally.

The second task involves utilizing career information for ongoing learning. This requires graduates to acquire and apply career resources to develop connections within the workplace, society, and the economy. Continuous education and professional development help graduates stay relevant in their fields. Building a network of contacts can open opportunities for collaboration and career advancement.

Mentoring newcomers to build skills helps many professionals foster a collaborative environment, enhance their leadership abilities, and ensure their teams' and organizations' growth and success. Such actions contribute to sharing career knowledge and wisdom with long-term positive outcomes, such as fostering a supportive work culture, nurturing professional growth, and building strong interpersonal relationships.

Mentorship plays a crucial role in shaping the career trajectories of individuals, promoting growth and development in both personal and professional capacities. The general economy benefits when mentors guide mentees to integrate their skills into their career planning, contributing to economic, social, and employment changes. For instance, a mentor might be an experienced professional in a specific industry, while the mentee could be a recent college graduate seeking guidance in navigating their career path.

Finally, new graduates can make vital lifelong decisions by taking charge of their future careers. They can connect, engage, and combine practical decision-making with career-building.

Employers have many expectations for graduates. The frustrating part is that what employers often expect needs to be more readily available, well-defined, and direct. Employers seek graduates who can seamlessly integrate into their workplace, demonstrate problem-solving skills, and adapt quickly to new challenges. They also expect graduates to possess a blend of technical expertise and soft skills, such as communication and teamwork. Understanding these expectations can help you, as a new graduate, better prepare for the demands of the professional world and increase success in your career.

Employers expect graduates to be quick thinkers, but it's tough! It takes practice and real-life situations to master. The real test comes when we're under pressure to perform, whether finishing tasks, collaborating with others, or communicating effectively. When in doubt, it's okay to ask questions.

First, never assume anything while interacting with your supervisor. When you ask a supervisor to repeat a question, you buy yourself enough time to respond adequately at best. If you realize you don't have an answer right away, suggest to your supervisor that you provide the information after your current engagement with them is finished. Consider the value of the different types of people from various backgrounds at work and be ready to ask questions when you need answers.

Second, always aim to be thoroughly prepared. Time management is crucial for success, so use tools like a calendar or to-do list to stay organized. Utilize an alarm clock to ensure you wake up on time and allocate enough time for tasks. Additionally, seek guidance from someone skilled in the organization if needed.

Third, work on organizing your thoughts effectively. This skill is essential for clear communication and decision-making in the workplace, especially if you tend to procrastinate. Take your time to think before speaking, as thoughtful communication is critical to success in any endeavor.

Fourth, project confidence! Your attire plays a significant role in how confident you appear. Dressing professionally can boost your self-assurance and leave a positive impression on others. Choose clothing that fits well and is appropriate for the workplace, reflecting your professionalism and attention to detail.

Fifth, practicing affirmations daily can also help boost your confidence and mental outlook. By consistently reinforcing positive beliefs about yourself, you can foster a more optimistic mindset and enhance your resilience in facing challenges.

Sixth, before speaking out confidently, take a moment to summarize what you want to express mentally and regularly check in with yourself to ensure clarity. Keep sentences simple and seek feedback frequently. Over time, you'll become adept at these skills.

Finally, lead from within by taking initiative during group projects or volunteering for small tasks, demonstrating confidence in your abilities and proactive contribution to the team.

Employers want graduates who can convert intellect to value. There is a difference between intellect and intelligence. Intellect is how a person can adequately describe a scenario by connecting it to *facts* to make sense. Conversely, intelligence is when a person can use *feelings* to connect to *facts*. Actor Matt Damon, superstar Shaquille O'Neal, and comedian Dave Chapelle are a few people who come to mind with high intellect. For example, Shaquille O'Neal successfully connected his role as a professional basketball superstar to that of a law enforcement officer, musician, actor, professional wrestler, businessman, and inventor. O'Neal, who earned his doctorate from Barry University in Miami, is a testament to his intellect (O'Neal, 2012).

Understanding our value is crucial as we navigate the professional world, much like the skills of Presidents Barack Obama (Ong, Burrow, & Fuller-Rowell, 2012) and Ronald Reagan (Meyer, 1990) in blending emotions with facts. We must Meticulously assess every line on our resumes and portfolios, ensuring they accurately reflect our intellect and worth. Take the time to estimate the value of each statement, comparing it to others with similar backgrounds and experiences to gauge your standing in the competitive landscape. Above all, seize every opportunity to demonstrate your skills to your supervisor. Seek feedback regularly and strive to learn something new each day.

Employers want graduates who are innovative and try new approaches to work. Generally, some people may be afraid to try new ways of working on and completing a task. Some individuals may hesitate to experiment with new methods for fear of failure or reluctance to deviate from familiar routines. This reluctance often stems from the tendency to rely on tried-and-true solutions that have proven effective in the past. You must understand that experience, as many people know it, can limit new opportunities! Some employers think that years of experience in a field don't automatically make someone an expert. They worry that long-time workers might need to learn new or improved methods. My advice is simple: actively seek out new connections. Engage with people at events, such as conferences, seminars, or workshops, to expand your knowledge and understanding, paving the way for personal and professional growth. Be vulnerable enough to explore a new talent and idea that you never knew you had.

Learning never stops! (Bendick, 2014). Especially for introverts, it's crucial to push yourself beyond your comfort zone to be sociable, friendly, and outgoing at work (Kahnweiler, 2015). The pandemic has been a constant reminder to be bolder, more intentional, and optimistic, showing that learning is an ongoing process.

Time has taught me the importance of breaking up the routine in both work and personal life. I refuse to settle for the mundane; when boredom creeps in, I make it my mission to find new and better ways of doing things. Growing as a person means facing fear and failure head-on and seeking inspiration from successful individuals who have overcome obstacles. I challenge myself to explore different areas of improvement and push my boundaries by regularly trying new activities and experiences.

Whether I'm learning a new sport, traveling solo, or even participating in professional speed dating, I embrace opportunities to step out of my comfort zone and recharge my creative energy. Employers desire flexible, adaptable graduates receptive to positive change in the work environment. If you direct your adaptive personality as a competitive advantage for your team, you will be viewed more as an asset to your employer. Being flexible means understanding there is room for improvement. Adaptability means being receptive to change and becoming a better leader in your career.

Openness to change is crucial for personal and professional growth. The perspective of change allows you the power to gauge and break the routine of work, offering fresh opportunities to improve. Embracing change means challenging beliefs and values while navigating various situations. Change allows you to appreciate the diversity and richness of your work and personal life. Along your journey, you'll discover how to leverage your strengths in the workplace, become more self-aware of the power of change, and appreciate how it can elevate your compassion.

Now, to some of you, what I am about to say may disappoint you. Do you know why? While you may have exhibited your intellectual abilities by maintaining high grades throughout your academic life, GPAs mean very little to some employers. Instead, employers expect graduates to demonstrate a range of intellectual abilities that extend beyond grades. According to Olson and Riordan (2012), in their report *Engage to Excel: Producing One Million Additional College Graduates with Degrees in Science, Technology, Engineering, and Mathematics*, many employers recognize that college graduates today are excelling academically at levels higher than ever before in history. However, despite this academic success, employers are also increasingly seeking nonacademic traits—such as adaptability, communication skills, and emotional intelligence—that are critical to thriving in the modern workplace. These skills often play an equally significant role in shaping a well-rounded and effective professional. As a result, the expectation of achieving an excellent GPA is not enough to bring to the table.

Employers always want more and prefer graduates with strong GPAs and other non-academic skill sets, such as effective communication (Bullen, Kordecki & Capener, 2020). As a result, expect to demonstrate how you can solve complex situations with minimal resources. It is also important to expect an assessment of your work and fit in the organization by coworkers. Whether the organization you work for provides training or not, you will be challenged to learn quickly with the expectation of success as a contributor.

Employees are expected to exhibit analytical skills, make decisions during unforeseen circumstances in the workplace, and display comfortability in resolving concrete, tangible, short-term objectives compared to more abstract, conceptual, and long-term objectives.

On the matter of decision-making, many employers particularly want to know whether you are:

1. Decisive, quick, thorough, or slow in making decisions;
2. Intuitive to make decisions based on *"gut feeling"* or prefer to lean towards facts;
3. Collaborative and involve others to make decisions;
4. Informed to make decisions based on past choices; and
5. Comfortable with making decisions that are aligned with your principles.

Employers keenly monitor graduates' creativity and intellectual alertness as they process systems, methods, products, structures, and services. Employees who master these traits are better positioned to progress quicker through the ranks in the workplace (Kavanaugh & Drennan, 2008).

Employers seek inquisitive graduates who are purposely and genuinely curious about workplace activities that pose positive results. Julie Winkle Giulioni, an award-winning author and learning and development practitioner, and Dr. Beverly Kaye, an internationally recognized leader in career development, employee engagement, and retention expert, offer six essential practices to connect inquisitive behaviors to actions for fulfilling workplace needs. These fancy, catchy phrases include relinquish control, jettison judgment, expect surprises from the team, gag the "fix it" reflex, embrace ignorance, and woo the cue (Kaye & Giulioni, 2012). The six practices are as follows:

1. Relinquish control suggests that leaders ask questions while trusting their employees to find the answers. Graduates invited to solve problems are encouraged to display leadership qualities by drawing upon prior knowledge, skills, and abilities.

2. Jettison judgment proposes that optimistic employers reject a toxic, judgmental culture in the work environment. They should make sound decisions after considering all inputs from all factions.

3. Expect surprises from the team. Transformative leaders are known to expect an element of creativity and innovation with an open-minded approach to receiving new information while interacting with employees. They thrive in learning new valuable ways to grow and benefit the company. While in this environment, it is vital to share nuanced information with your supervisor.

4. Gag the "fix it" reflex. This practice highlights the can-do spirit of managers. While there are many roles a supervisor has, one is to fix problems. Many supervisors appreciate the can-do spirit of their employees rather than feel threatened. To solve problems, employees may need to delegate tasks. In my experience, I have

realized that there are two ways to appreciate problems: *fix* the problem or *understand* the situation. However, not all issues need fixing. Some require a genuine curiosity to appreciate the complexities that make it problematic. Be open to opportunities to show your abilities and skill sets. Some people will earn the diploma but have no idea how to leverage their skill sets after graduating.

5. Embracing ignorance is decentralized knowledge. Transformative supervisors understand that embracing ignorance helps breed a thriving culture where knowledge flows in the workplace. Fear not of your lack of work knowledge, skills, and abilities. Communicate your limitations. Optics is everything, especially at work. Project to your supervisor your willingness to learn despite constraints.

6. Woo the cue highlights how employers find creative ways to seek and utilize information previously unavailable. Graduates should be

excited to work with employers with a record of hiring and retaining managers who constantly seek new ways to engage their subordinates to bring the best out of their employees. Graduates should ask questions to get the correct information about organizations before applying. The person who creates new ideas brings value to the workplace. Take that bold step.

At the end of the day, remember that knowledge of these skills is money for those who know its worth. *People are willing to pay a premium for value.*

Success often comes to those who can effectively translate their expertise into tangible outcomes. It is not just about what you know, but how you apply the listed skills and the knowledge from your earned degrees to solve real-world problems. The ability to continuously learn and adapt is what sets the most successful individuals apart from the rest.

Holistic Innovation.

Every company tier requires innovation, which is not easy or cheap. Employers want innovative graduates. Some people with innovation resources protect it until they are comfortable sharing that information with others. To be creative, graduates must hone three behavioral competencies: personal effectiveness and academic and workplace competencies.

First, personal effectiveness means graduates learn and act on the skills, rendering them true professionals. This foundation of competence and reliability is what enables them to consistently deliver high-quality results in their chosen fields.

Second, academic competencies emphasize the importance of communicating professionalism through reading, writing, listening, and critical and analytical skills. These abilities are essential for navigating complex challenges and conveying ideas effectively in a professional setting.

Third, workplace competencies reflect the balance of work and life. Graduates must sharpen these three behavioral competencies during their first 90 days of hire. Cultivating these skills not only helps in immediate job performance but also sets the foundation for long-term career growth and adaptability in a rapidly changing job market.

Holistic innovation in the workplace is about more than groundbreaking ideas or inventing the next big thing. It is also about how we carry ourselves and interact with others. As graduates enter a new organization, workplace expectations beyond our academic competencies include personal effectiveness and workplace competencies. These behavioral competencies require graduates to know how to become a team player, plan and organize at work, and problem-solve. For graduates to fine-tune their competencies, they must assess their self-awareness level and be courageous by sharing ideas that add value to an organization.

Graduates must demand support for their intellectual growth and, in the process, urge their supervisors to learn new tools, technology included, to improve work efforts. As graduates, you must advocate for opportunities that foster your intellectual growth. For instance, you can request access to professional development resources or propose training sessions on emerging technologies relevant to your field. Additionally, you can encourage your supervisors to stay updated on industry advancements and consider implementing new tools or software that streamline workflow and enhance productivity.

Logical Thinking.

Employers expect graduates to have strong logical skills. For example, employees must exhibit clear and sound actions, especially within a diverse work environment. This trait is a prized jewel at the workplace, as understanding processes can have various meanings for people. A graduate who appreciates the importance of logic in communicating effectively will almost guarantee a successful professional life where coworkers don't feel snubbed, slighted, or disrespected. Mastering logical skills may require graduates to try new approaches to improving their memory and clear thinking. For some, this may be journaling their plans, reading fiction, playing games, and creating new adventures.

Critical Thinking.

Critical thinking skills, a subset of logical thinking, are wide-ranging and incorporate the ability to observe scenarios, analyze situations, interpret probes, reflect on contexts, evaluate feedback, infer how changes affect outcomes, explain consequences, problem-solve complex facts, and make decisions that influence change. Employees desire graduates who are critical thinkers. Carl Jung, a Swiss psychiatrist and psychoanalyst, famously stated that thinking is complex, leading most people to judge.

Employers prefer to hire and retain graduates who know how to ask relatable questions rather than judge based on generalizations. They fancy graduates who question basic assumptions through personal beliefs and biases. Developing strong critical thinking skills is being aware of your thoughts and perceptions. Understand that no one thinks critically 100 percent of the time. Nobody is perfect. However, striving to be a critical thinker as much as possible is essential.

Creative Thinking.

Employers highly seek out creative graduates. The famous physicist Albert Einstein once said, "Creativity is intelligence having fun" (Demarin & Derke, 2020). What a way to see the world through creativity! Creativity, associated with enjoyment, stimulates ideas for projects. While copyrighting or patenting can be expensive, protecting and preserving your ideas is worth the shot. In the workplace, use your creativity to generate new ideas that could benefit your team. Be known for leaving a legacy with this approach.

When you work in teams, broaden your knowledge base by requesting certification opportunities and courses on subjects within your area of expertise. Many professional development opportunities are funded through an employer. However, this is dependent on the budget. Whether or not your department has sufficient money allocated to invest in your training, do not despair. Have your requests in writing that you are interested in such opportunities. Provide a copy of the request you filed as part of your employment records.

Throughout your time in the position, make sure to join diverse teams, adding to its creative collaboration, while planning to mention to your supervisor at the opportune time to:

1. **Hire** professionals and volunteers who are creative thinkers. When suggesting new hires, emphasize the importance of creativity and innovation in problem-solving.

2. **Create** an inspiring and enjoyable work environment. Consider adding colorful artwork or comfortable seating areas to the office to boost creativity, comfortability, and morale.

3. **Acknowledge and reward** creative ideas. Implement a system where employees receive recognition or bonuses for innovative solutions or suggestions.

4. **Offer** resources to help teams prevent and manage stress effectively. Provide access to meditation apps or organize stress-relief workshops for employees to attend.

5. **Lead** by example by demonstrating creativity for your team members to emulate. Incorporate creative thinking exercises into team meetings or share examples of innovative projects you've worked on.

Encouraging creative and bold leadership, especially in a fun way, can help you and your team succeed by thinking creatively (otherwise referred to as lateral thinking) and finding unique solutions to problems.

Lateral Thinking.

Employers desire graduates who think laterally. Lateral thinking is a fundamental professional skill beneficial for solving problems directly and indirectly (Aithal & Kumar, 2016). To laterally think, a graduate must solicit support from experienced colleagues by asking unusual questions. It is okay for such questions to be strange, odd, curious, extraordinary, abnormal, remarkable, bizarre, and atypical. These questions intend to find practical and rational solutions in nuanced ways. Lateral thinking requires experience that new graduates may still need to gain. Instead, graduates with limited experience must seek skilled and "seasoned" professionals as mentors. Companies require lateral thinking to solve complex problems in new, innovative ways.

Furthermore, lateral thinking requires you to use your imagination to look at a problem differently from how you previously viewed problems and present a new solution that piques the team's imagination. A graduate in a management role shall most certainly need to draw on lateral thinking skills to solve problems and lead the team in all aspects of problem-solving. In other words, lateral thinking is solving a problem using an unusual or creative approach not previously used. Coming from the biblical canon, the character King Solomon's decision to propose dividing the child between two women is a classic example of lateral thinking (New King James Version, 1982, 1 Kings 3:16-28). By employing this unconventional method, Solomon was able to reveal the true mother, demonstrating the power of creative problem-solving. Philosopher Edward de Bono coined lateral thinking in his 1985 book *Six Thinking Hats* (de Bono, 1985).

Skill Advancement and Earning Potential.

Graduates should be aware that pursuing further education and training opportunities is crucial for enhancing their skills and remaining competitive in the job market. Specialized certification programs, online courses from reputable institutions, and attending industry-related conferences can significantly contribute to career success. Consider enrolling in specialized certification programs tailored to your interest or exploring online courses from reputable institutions. Attending industry-related conferences and networking events also provides valuable insights and connections to help you succeed in your career.

In Torpey's (2019) analysis, professional development opportunities play a critical role in achieving high wages and substantial financial rewards. Nurse anesthetists earn the highest annual wages of over $165,000 with little or no career experience within ten years. This fact is crucial for aspiring healthcare professionals to understand as it highlights the potential for substantial financial reward and career advancement in the field of nurse anesthesia, even at the early stages of their careers. The master's-level occupations shown in BLS Table 2 below showed the seven highest paying occupations projected for 2016 through 2026. Connecting these insights to professional development, it becomes evident that pursuing specialized training and advanced degrees can significantly enhance earning potential and career prospects.

Table 2. Highest paying occupations that typically require a master's degree for entry, 2017

Occupation	Median annual wage, 2017 [1]	Work experience in a related occupation	On-the-job training	Occupational openings, projected 2016–26 annual average
Nurse anesthetists	$165,120	None	None	2,800
Political scientists	115,110	None	None	700
Computer and information research scientists	114,520	None	None	2,500
Physician assistants	104,860	None	None	10,600
Nurse practitioners	103,880	None	None	14,400
Mathematicians	103,010	None	None	300
Economists	102,490	None	None	1,600

[1] Data exclude wages of self-employed workers.
Source: U.S. Bureau of Labor Statistics, Office of Occupational Statistics and Employment Projections.

Source: Torpey (2019).

Employers want graduates who can conceptualize issues quickly. Like lateral thinking, conceptualizing issues rapidly requires experience. In college, you might have taken courses that required you to use abstract and original ideas to solve problems. Original ideas to solve problems are appreciated. To nurture a creative flow of ideas, return to lessons learned during college, including the hypothetical and theoretical concepts and case studies or project management models to identify and solve problems to break down and understand why things happen the way they do.

As you navigate the realities of today's job market, it's essential to pair your passion and practical career strategies with keen observational skills in the workplace.

Table 3. Highest paying occupations that typically require a bachelor's degree for entry, 2017

Occupation	Median annual wage, 2017 [1]	Work experience in a related occupation	On-the-job training	Occupational openings, projected 2016–26 annual average
Chief executives	$183,270	5 years or more	None	20,000
Computer and information systems managers	139,220	5 years or more	None	32,500
Architectural and engineering managers	137,720	5 years or more	None	13,600
Airline pilots, copilots, and flight engineers	137,930	Less than 5 years	Moderate term	8,100
Petroleum engineers	132,280	None	None	2,800
Marketing managers	132,230	5 years or more	None	21,300
Financial managers	125,080	5 years or more	None	56,900

[1] Data exclude wages of self-employed workers.
Source: U.S. Bureau of Labor Statistics, Office of Occupational Statistics and Employment Projections.

Source: Torpey (2019).

When considering the realities of today's job market, recent graduates must approach their career choices with a mindset that balances passion and practicality. A degree is undoubtedly a powerful tool for opening doors, but relying solely on its academic value is not enough to ensure long-term success. The U.S. Department of Labor and major job platforms like *LinkedIn* and *Indeed* provide a wealth of data on which industries are offering the most job opportunities for bachelor's degree holders. These sources identify high-demand fields like computer systems management, engineering, marketing, and finance, with salaries ranging from $28,000 to $56,900 annually. However, many of these roles also require work experience to truly capitalize on their earning potential, and obtaining these jobs often involves strategic lateral thinking—like the workplace redesign suggested by Joel Ratekin to foster both collaboration and productivity (Shukla, 2016).

While these opportunities are enticing, graduates must also be aware that success is not guaranteed by academic credentials alone. The value of further education and training cannot be overstated; it is essential for remaining competitive in an ever-evolving job market. Pursuing further learning opportunities also nurtures your personal growth, which, in turn, enhances your overall effectiveness in the workplace. As Saurabh Shukla's lateral thinking example shows, success often comes from innovation and a willingness to rethink traditional approaches to problem-solving, rather than merely following a set path. This dynamic mindset, paired with passion and personal development, will be more sustainable than focusing solely on monetary gain. This strategy not only opens the door to financial stability but also ensures that your career remains aligned with your passions, leading to greater fulfillment over the long term.

Now, reflect on your role in your current environment, closely watching how your supervisors or leaders assess situations and make decisions. By understanding their use of lateral thinking and problem-solving, you can begin to apply these concepts to your own professional development. Whether it's through internal meetings, external seminars, or networking events, this skill can significantly enhance your ability to thrive in competitive industries.

Pursuing Advanced Degrees.

In the competitive landscape of today's job market, employers are increasingly looking for candidates who not only possess advanced degrees but also demonstrate a deep commitment to their field. The pursuit of a doctoral, professional, or terminal degree, while challenging, signifies a candidate's dedication to becoming a subject-matter expert. This elevated level of expertise is often what employers desire, as it places graduates among a distinguished group of professionals who have invested significant time and effort to achieve their credentials.

For instance, the medical profession serves as a prime example of how advanced qualifications align with employer expectations. Medical professionals — ranging from primary care providers to researchers — are expected to continuously refine their skills, communicate effectively, and solve complex problems collaboratively. These attributes are critical in fulfilling their essential roles and meeting the increasing demands of the healthcare industry. Employers in the medical field highly value these qualities, recognizing that they contribute to exceptional patient care and ongoing advancements in medical practice.

Although the Bureau of Labor Statistics (BLS) Occupational Employment Statistics program does not announce earnings for occupations with a median annual wage more significant than or equal to $208,000, Table 1 shows the seven highest-paying occupations in the medical profession from 2016 to 2026. Anesthesiology is the highest, obtained upon completion of internship or residency. About 1,400 openings are expected to be available between 2016 and 2026. Of the top seven medical professionals, general practitioners have the least earnings.

What employers want is not only specialized knowledge and expertise but also a demonstrated commitment to ongoing professional development and excellence. This chapter highlights how achieving advanced degrees and cultivating essential skills align with employer expectations, ultimately leading to higher career prospects and fulfilling professional roles.

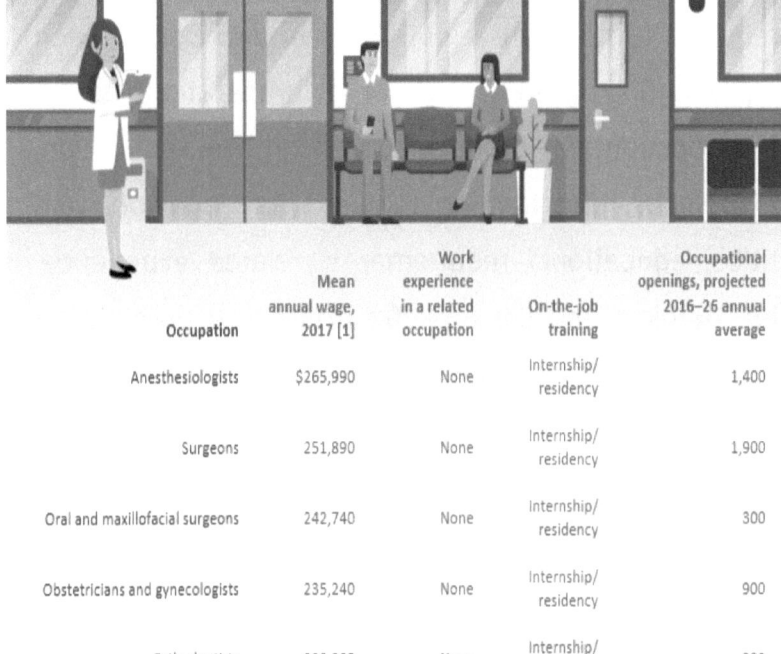

Occupation	Mean annual wage, 2017 [1]	Work experience in a related occupation	On-the-job training	Occupational openings, projected 2016–26 annual average
Anesthesiologists	$265,990	None	Internship/ residency	1,400
Surgeons	251,890	None	Internship/ residency	1,900
Oral and maxillofacial surgeons	242,740	None	Internship/ residency	300
Obstetricians and gynecologists	235,240	None	Internship/ residency	900
Orthodontists	229,380	None	Internship/ residency	300
Psychiatrists	216,090	None	Internship/ residency	1,100
Family and general practitioners	208,560	None	Internship/ residency	5,600

[1] Data exclude wages of self-employed workers. The Occupational Employment Statistics program does not publish wages for occupations with a median annual wage that is greater than or equal to $208,000. Occupations in this category include most doctoral and professional degree-level occupations. Therefore, mean wages are shown.

Source: U.S. Bureau of Labor Statistics, Office of Occupational Statistics and Employment Projections.

Source: Torpey (2019).

A Job Zone is a classification system used by the U.S. Department of Labor to categorize occupations based on the level of education, experience, and training required to perform a job. The five Job Zones, each representing different levels of job preparation, feature five occupation groups based on the education, experience, and training required for each job. Job titles, educational requirements, related experience, job training, and the Specific Vocational Preparation (SVP) range are within each Job Zone. O*NET OnLine, accessible at https://www.onetonline.org/, is an invaluable resource for graduates exploring job zones.

This online platform offers comprehensive insights into various occupations, aiding graduate job seekers, workforce development professionals, HR personnel, students, researchers, veterans, and more. Providing detailed descriptions of job tasks, required technology skills, tools utilized, preferred knowledge, skills, and abilities, and in-depth information on work activities, this website is tailored to help you effectively navigate the workforce.

SVPs, ranging from 1 to 5, are provided, indicating the time needed to learn the necessary skills for an average job performance. The website also provides insights into educational backgrounds, credentials, interests, work styles, values, and wages, all crucial aspects to consider when exploring potential career paths. While on this website, use the *"Occupation Quick Search"* tab to search for your occupation of choice. During the search, you will find an array of professions that closely match your desired option. You may also be provided with *"Bright Outlook"* occupations. These occupations are expected to grow over time, with more job openings over several years.

New graduates can explore burgeoning areas in the future by considering "green" careers, which are any occupations designed to protect and improve the environment. Green careers include positions to conserve or develop alternative energy, reduce pollution, and recycle. Jobs in the green economy are rising, impacting how we work, the skills we need, and even customer expectations. For instance, agriculture, forestry, and energy management are shifting towards eco-friendly practices, like using natural pesticides or focusing on energy efficiency. Government, construction, and manufacturing sectors also embrace green initiatives, creating new opportunities for those interested in sustainable careers.

So, *How do you like them future "apples"?* Reflect on the following questions: *How prepared do you currently feel about your chances to succeed? How do you tell your supervisor you are best suited for an open position?* There are many ways to look at these questions. Specifically, you demonstrate how you delivered results from your previous work experience, including college. Your supervisor must know you have a combination of skills and experiences, making you stand out. Any good manager would appreciate your knowledge, expertise, work ethic, and other qualities that propel you to stand out as an employee. Share your aligned vision, goals, and mission with your supervisor and team. A strong supervisor will appreciate this quality in an employee who fulfills their duties effectively and shares their goals and aspirations for the company's success.

Specifically, demonstrate how you deliver results from your previous work and college experience. Remember, your presence in a company has nothing to do with good grades and success in college or triumph with a former employer. Instead, your supervisor must know you have the skills and experience to be exceptional. Any good manager would appreciate your knowledge, expertise, work ethic, and other qualities that propel you to stand out as an employee.

In Chapter 3, we will dive into soft skills, the fluffy pillows of your career success! Think of soft skills as the marshmallows in your hot cocoa – essential for that perfect blend of professionalism and warmth. In this chapter, we will unravel the mysteries of communication, teamwork, and adaptability, showing you how to juggle all three like a pro circus performer. So, grab your popcorn and get ready for a rollercoaster ride through the delightful realm of career skills!

CHAPTER 3

Soft skills? What is that? ...

"Soft skills get little respect but they will make or break your career" (Bertelsen, n.d.).

Peggy Klaus

Best-selling author, communication and leadership coach, and political consultant Peggy Klaus has worked with companies such as Credit Suisse, Disney, UNICEF, and Kaiser Permanente. Author of *BRAG! The Art of Tooting Your Own Horn Without Blowing It*, Klaus is regularly featured in the Today Show, 20/20, BusinessWeek, Wall Street Journal, New York Times, and O Magazine. She has also lectured at Harvard, UC Berkeley, and Wharton.

When embarking on your journey into the professional world, you may be bombarded with advice about the importance of technical skills, degrees, certifications, and micro credentials. But amidst the noise, allow Peggy Klaus's words to ring loud and clear: *"Soft skills get little respect, but they will make or break your career"* (Bertelsen, n.d.). It is a statement that cuts through the clutter and forces you to reevaluate what truly matters in the workplace.

In this chapter, we explore why soft skills — such as communication, teamwork, and problem-solving — are essential components of career success that often receive less attention compared to technical expertise. While technical skills and formal qualifications like degrees and certifications are important for demonstrating your capabilities, soft skills are crucial for navigating the complexities of the workplace and building effective relationships. Employers increasingly value these interpersonal skills because they directly impact productivity, collaboration, and overall job satisfaction.

Soft skills enhance your ability to apply technical knowledge in real-world scenarios, fostering a positive and productive work environment. This chapter will delve into the ways in which soft skills complement technical proficiency and why developing them is imperative for career advancement and achieving long-term professional success.

Finally, the chapter also delves into the often-overlooked realm of soft skills – those intangible qualities that shape how you interact with others, navigate challenges, and, ultimately, define your success. So, what exactly are soft skills, and why are they essential for thriving in your new field? Let's unravel the mystery together and uncover the keys to unlocking your full potential in the professional world.

Defining Soft Skills.

The ability to smile effortlessly, speak to others warmly, offer suggestions, and manage time effectively represents soft skills. Soft skills are qualities or interpersonal gifts that influence your ability to work and interact with others. While soft skills are required across industries and job types, they are seldom taught in college.

Only recently, numerous four-year colleges needed more dedicated courses preparing graduates for the workplace, and even if these courses existed, they often needed more robust support and enthusiasm. Yet, it is refreshing to note that the push for several colleges for their graduates to cultivate "people" skills is gathering momentum. It is equally cool to see the number of professional organizations taking steps to push this agenda.

Many colleges realize that providing graduates with exemplary "people" skills is a great marketing tool for recruitment. Soft skills are now related more to emotional intelligence to improve graduates' abilities on a new level. In response to the evolving demands of the modern workforce, colleges recognize the role of soft skills in shaping the success of their graduates.

Beyond academic achievement, cultivating emotional and social intelligence quotients and interpersonal abilities is essential.

By focusing on "people" skills, colleges not only enhance the employability of their graduates but also position themselves as attractive options for prospective students. This shift in mindset represents a paradigmatic change in higher education, where the holistic development of students is prioritized, empowering their navigation of the world's complexities with confidence and competence.

Social (Soft) Skills.

Social skills refer to your ability to interact effectively and harmoniously with others in various social and professional settings. It involves communication, empathy, teamwork, and adaptability, which are crucial for building relationships and succeeding in your career (MacLeod, 2016).

Before stepping into the workforce, practicing and refining your interpersonal skills is essential. Start by actively listening to others and engaging in conversations. Take opportunities to collaborate on group projects or join clubs and organizations where you can interact with diverse groups of people (River, 2023). This will help you develop empathy and communication skills valued in professional environments.

Building interpersonal skills begins with stepping out of your comfort zone and approaching interactions with an open mind. According to Gibson, Hardy, and Buckley (2014), practice introducing yourself confidently and engaging in small talk. Remember to ask open-ended questions to show genuine interest in others. Networking events and informational interviews are excellent opportunities to practice these skills and expand your professional network.

While improving your interpersonal skills, staying authentic and accurate to yourself is essential. Be genuine in your interactions and values, as people are more likely to connect with someone sincere. Recognize your strengths and areas for growth and use them to build relationships that align with your personal and career aspirations (Carson, 2023).

Start by acknowledging and accepting your feelings if you're naturally shy or socially awkward. Gradually expose yourself to social situations that challenge you but at a comfortable pace (White, 2023). Practice positive self-talk and focus on your strengths rather than perceived weaknesses. Seek supportive environments and consider joining groups or workshops to boost confidence and social skills.

These tips and strategies will help recent graduates develop essential social skills and navigate the complexities of interpersonal relationships in both personal and professional settings.

Interpersonal (Soft) Skills.

Interpersonal skills are used daily as you interact and communicate with people, including co-workers and management. These skills are vital for people who work in customer service, realty, or financial planning. As a college grad, good interpersonal skills lead to career success. The knowledge of interpersonal skills can help you build relationships, maintain strong connections, and gain respect from colleagues. Plus, it can help you establish yourself as a leader and showcase your skills.

It is essential to communicate effectively with people, especially in a professional setting or in a social one. Lacking strong interpersonal skills can make it challenging to make connections and find success in your career. According to Goleman (2006), good interpersonal skills can help you be more successful in the workplace since they can help you build relationships, establish trust, and show respect for the people you work with.

According to Browne (2019), having interpersonal skills helps you to understand how to interact with people and build long-term relationships. Reiman (2007) adds that listening and responding to others is vital for success in the modern workplace. Finally, Deutschendorf (2009) emphasizes that strong interpersonal skills can help create a positive work culture and environment. So, focus on developing your interpersonal skills to succeed in your career.

The Problem and the Need for Soft Skills.

As I started my journey into the world of work, I had all the technical skills one could want, but I felt like I needed help. When I stumbled upon Peggy Klaus's wise words: *"Soft skills get little respect, but they will make or break your career,"* it was like a light bulb moment! Communication, understanding emotions, flexibility, and working well with others were super important. Like a big brother or sister guiding me, I set out to learn and practice these soft skills. It wasn't just about getting a job—it was about becoming the kind of person who could handle anything the workplace threw my way with confidence and ease. And so, armed with Klaus's advice, I embarked on an exciting journey, ready to tackle whatever challenges came my way.

As a recent graduate, understanding the REAL challenges you face at the workplace has little or no bearing on your excellent GPA. Add the real challenges here. Such problems affect many areas of the graduate's professional development. They need to be equipped with the necessary soft skills for success in the workforce. For the most part, character attributes such as chronic tardiness, inappropriate clothing, a display of tattoos, gossip, and a sullen attitude are not brought to their attention as unacceptable habits on campuses, at internship and externship sites, and certainly not in work environments.

Negative attitudes of graduates as new employees, such as ignoring coworkers intentionally, devoting efforts only to assigned work without initiative, and habitually staying on mobile devices for personal use, are everyday occurrences. Wearing headphones and relying solely on electronic messaging at work might not convey a strong appreciation for verbal and interpersonal skills in the office. It is important to consider how this behavior might be perceived, as it could unintentionally signal a lack of interest in understanding the company culture, learning about opportunities, and getting to know your coworkers, potentially leading to negative consequences.

The resurgence of social justice movements, particularly among young people, mirrors similar movements in America's past. Research supports this trend, such as the work by Deron Boyles, Tony Carusi, and Dennis Attick in *Handbook of Social Justice in Education*, which underscores the pivotal role of younger generations in advocating for social change (Boyles, Carusi, & Attick, 2009). School-age children and college students are at the forefront of these movements. This is evidenced by Shawn Ginwright, Julio Cammarota, and Pedro Noguera's peer-reviewed article, "Youth, Social Justice, and Communities:

Toward a Theory of Urban Youth Policy." Their activism reflects an increasing awareness and commitment to addressing social justice issues in contemporary society (Ginwright et al., 2005).

In today's digital age, young graduates, regardless of their racial backgrounds, are increasingly aware of the challenges facing people of color and other vulnerable communities. However, many graduates may need help addressing these social issues in various professional settings, including job interviews, virtual meetings, company gatherings, and everyday interactions.

Some employers prefer to avoid engaging in these topics, but some do. Emotional and social intelligence and common sense are valuable soft skills that can help you turn these challenges into opportunities for positive change. Emotional intelligence involves understanding and managing your emotions and empathizing with others, while social intelligence is about navigating social situations effectively and building strong relationships. Combined with common sense, these skills can empower you to address social issues with empathy and wisdom, fostering meaningful change in your professional and personal life. It is imperative to know when to engage in these topics at the workplace using intelligence quotient techniques. Always use your better instincts to navigate these delicate issues.

The expectations of employers for graduates to be well-equipped with soft skills are very high. Successful professionals understand that for them to succeed, soft skills have a role to play in their realization of better opportunities for upward mobility and more meaningful careers that benefit their families and organizations. These expectations are as severe, intentional, and real now as ever before. Thankfully, many higher education institutions and employers address these problems by designing ways to improve the soft skills of college students. For some colleges, several creative public and corporate engagements have been considered to align with corporate sponsorship to provide professional development programs for faculty and students.

In the 21st century, many essential skills are developed through project-based learning, which is highly valued by today's employers (Pawar, Kulkarni & Patil, 2020). These skills include collaborating effectively with others, resolving interpersonal conflicts, making thoughtful decisions, and tackling complex problems. These abilities are crucial for completing projects in the workplace while maintaining their value.

Extensive research has been conducted to determine which soft skills are most critical for employers in the 21st century. Researchers like Yurii Pelekh of the University of Rzeszow in Poland and Ganna Shlikhta from Rivne State University of the Humanities, Ukraine, have delved into the significance of soft skills in today's job market (Pelekh & Shlikhta, 2024). Similarly, Ana Maria Lara-Palma and her research team, authors of the *21st Century Skills: What Else* article, have explored the evolving landscape of essential skills for success. Through their studies, it becomes evident that communication is a paramount soft skill demanded by employers across diverse fields and industries in the modern era (Lara-Palma et al., 2022).

Across various industries, communication consistently emerges as the top soft skill. Communication serves as the cornerstone upon which other skills are built. Soft skills such as adaptability to different schedules, a positive work attitude, responsibility, self-confidence, time management, resilience, social appropriateness, and teamwork all hinge on effective communication. Therefore, understanding, appreciating, and embracing effective communication is essential for mastering these vital skills.

Communication as a Soft Skill.

You must always rely on practical verbal communication skills. I pride myself in this area. As a foreign-American, I work exceptionally hard to chisel off my foreign accent over time. As an educator in North America, I need to do that. Students should be able to handle my strong accent for their engagements with me. Listening abilities should be sharpened to reduce misunderstandings during any communication. Draw on your emotional intelligence skills to counter your valuable points when dealing with difficult situations. Building rapport with your negotiating partner to resolve middle-ground challenges would be best. Be assertive throughout the negotiations without appearing aloof, standoffish, or snobbish. Always keep an even tone of your voice. Smiles and eye contact is a requirement.

Communicating well is the best way to send and receive a clear message. This applies to everything you do in your workplace or personal life. You can convey a message effectively through speaking, writing, or body language. Effective oral and written communication is essential for management, human resources, aerospace, and sales careers. According to Debbie Ritchie, managing director of Huron's Studer

Group business, effective communication is a crucial skill that all leaders, regardless of their industry, must possess (Cochrane et al., 2019; Ritchie, 2018). For example, the fast-paced U.S. healthcare industry has made leaders accountable for communicating effectively. Better execution of tasks depends almost singularly on how clear the *"why,"* *"what,"* and *"how"* information is to others to perform as directed. When employers lead with a clear understanding of the *"why,"* the *"what,"* and the *"how,"* direction is no longer difficult. Successful communicators are clear about what they say or write and how they actively listen. A not-so-good communicator can find it challenging to articulate their thoughts and, in so doing, create misunderstanding among other staff, sponsors, customers, and interested parties.

As a brand-new graduate, the best way to master soft communication skills is to take the following simple rules seriously. First, show confidence when you speak and when you listen. Second, give respect; don't worry about earning it first. This can be tricky but be sure to exercise wisdom. Third, show genuine sympathy and empathy only when you can relate to the circumstances. Don't patronize your peers or customers; people can easily see through it, as many perceive it as an insult. Fourth, listen with all your "senses." Your ear should pay attention to words. Be careful when answering inquiries and questions with courtesy.

Fifth, communicate verbally by paying attention to your tone and cadence. At the workplace, cadence measures the frequency, format, and sequence patterns managers share with their team members, allowing employees to share their input in the regular course of work. Sixth, pay attention to messages you send other than by mouth or speech. You will be assessed based on nonverbal cues, such as body movements, posture, and facial expressions, which convey emotions like happiness, sadness, anger, surprise, fear, and disgust consistently.

This is especially difficult for people from various cultures entering a new culture with different social cues. Cultural ways of doing something only sometimes translate effectively in various social settings. Social cues are cultural signals that can vary significantly from one culture to another, making it essential to adapt and learn the nuances of social interactions in different cultural contexts.

Seventh, electronic and technical communication must be decisive and professional, including email, texts, hashtags, and hand-held transmitters. Eighth, take constructive feedback as a welcome opportunity to discover new ideas. And ninth, always have a friendly attitude. It is infectious when you become friendly. Others feel comfortable to work with and around you.

Teamwork as a Soft Skill.

Michael Jordan, the luminary NBA superstar and businessman, stated, *"Talent wins games, but teamwork and intelligence win championships"* (Miller, 2009, p. 30). For some, working in teams can be either fun or terrifying, depending on your personality. A social and outgoing employee may often work better with people in a way that a reclusive and shy employee may struggle with. Despite your personality traits, collaborating with others at some point in the company is required and expected. Working with others on a team allows you to engage well in a group while effectively completing tasks. Teamwork is necessary in any career, whether for event coordination, software engineering, market research, or any other aspect of building community within your occupation. Keep in mind that when working in a team, adopting an attitude of sharing credit for completing work is just as important.

No one creates a task entirely alone. In addition, when speaking up and sharing ideas, understand that feedback is inevitable when working in a team. Be satisfied even if your creative ideas are not implemented or accepted. As a teammate, the goal is to be open and welcoming to the people around you with a collaborative spirit. Never encourage selfish attitudes. A self-absorbed and negative attitude is a set-up for failure over time by an employee or employer. You may want to reconsider your employment if you notice negative attitudes and behaviors in the organization's culture.

Conflict Management as a Soft Skill.

At any given moment, anyone can find themselves conflicted about matters big or small. Especially at work, conflicts come in many forms. Task-related conflicts. Personality-based conflicts. Work-style conflicts. Conflicts around discrimination. Conflicts around social justice and politics. The list is long. Let's take leadership conflict, for example. Supervisors have different leadership styles, which are closely linked to how conflicts are managed. Some supervisors lead with boldness, courage, and charisma, which can inspire confidence but might also lead to clashes if not handled carefully.

Despite your supervisor's leadership style, your conflict management approach will be crucial in maintaining a positive and productive work environment. Whether they are bold and charismatic, laid-back and inviting, highly technical, or hands-off, adapting your conflict resolution strategies to align with their style can help you navigate challenges more effectively. This understanding will enable you to respond appropriately, fostering better communication and cooperation within the team.

Emphasizing a shared respect for differences helps prevent and resolve conflicts. Acknowledging and valuing diverse perspectives can create an inclusive environment where everyone feels heard and respected. This approach not only helps in smoothing out misunderstandings but also encourages collaboration and innovation. When you address conflicts with empathy and an open mind, you set a positive example for your peers and contribute to a more harmonious workplace. This fosters cultural respect and cooperation, which are essential for personal and professional growth.

How do you accomplish this goal? Start by actively listening to your colleagues and acknowledging their viewpoints. Show empathy by putting yourself in their shoes and understanding their feelings and perspectives. Communicate clearly and openly, ensuring that your messages are respectful and considerate. Encourage open dialogue and be willing to compromise when necessary. You can inspire others to do the same by modeling these behaviors, creating a more cohesive and productive team environment.

When should an employee communicate the following to their supervisor? Timing and context are crucial. Choose a moment when your supervisor is not overwhelmed with other tasks and can give you their full attention. It is best to schedule a meeting or catch them during a less busy time. Ensure you communicate your thoughts respectfully and constructively, focusing on solutions rather than problems. Avoid discussing sensitive issues in public or during high-stress moments, as this can lead to misunderstandings or defensiveness. By being mindful of when and how you communicate, you can effectively address concerns without risking your job or creating unnecessary tension.

Provide constructive feedback to your supervisor. Communicate to your supervisor how their leadership styles affect you by sharing how they interact with the work styles and personalities of people on their team and around them. Your transparency should help your supervisor connect with other employees, regardless of their leadership preferences. Embracing our differences can lead to a more inclusive and respectful workplace culture. This openness encourages everyone to take accountability for their actions and work together to resolve conflicts constructively. By fostering a culture of transparency and respect, you create an environment where all voices are heard, and everyone's contributions are valued.

Delegation as a Soft Skill.

For this discussion, understand that *managers* and *supervisors* mean the same thing and will be used interchangeably. On many occasions at work, effective managers complete tasks the team requires. Better managers complete tasks by sharing with others on the team for two reasons. Do some managers need to complete tasks without the team based on their roles and responsibilities? Yes, sometimes managers must handle specific tasks independently due to the nature of their roles. These tasks might involve sensitive information, strategic planning, or high-level decision-making that requires their expertise and authority.

Understanding when to work independently and when to affect the team is a crucial part of effective management. This balance ensures that individual and team efforts contribute to the organization's success.

Members can often accomplish tasks better with a team because collaboration brings diverse perspectives and skills together. When a team works together, they can brainstorm ideas, solve problems more efficiently, and support each other through challenges. Each member contributes unique strengths, making the team more effective than anyone working alone. This collaborative approach enhances the quality of work and fosters a sense of community and shared purpose within the organization.

Micromanaging people takes away trust. When managers constantly oversee every detail, it can make team members feel undervalued and stifled. Delegating or assigning tasks to team members who are more knowledgeable or skilled in a particular area is a leadership quality a supervisor or manager should embody. Delegation requires you to trust employees with responsibilities while ensuring that work is done well. Instead of fostering a collaborative environment, micromanagement can hinder creativity and independent thinking.

In a work setting, delegation generally means handing over responsibility for a task from a manager to a team member. Delegation is usually the supervisor's job, but you can offer to help with this role in a respectful way. This shows your initiative and can help you stand out when you seek a raise or promotion. Managers can build a more dynamic and innovative team by honoring each member's autonomy and trusting them to contribute their unique skills. This approach empowers individuals and promotes a culture of mutual respect and shared responsibility, where everyone feels invested in the project's success. Efficient managers lead by delegating tasks effectively, allowing team members to take ownership of their work, and encouraging a more productive and harmonious workplace.

Listening as a Soft Skill.

It is essential to listen carefully. In the workplace, listening helps you understand the needs of your colleagues and allows you to provide better solutions to the challenges you and your team may face. According to Brady-Myerov (2021), listening Is a lost art and an often-overlooked skill in the workplace, but critical to successful collaboration and effective problem-solving. As noted by Forbes contributor Dorie Clark (2014), when you actively listen to your colleagues, you demonstrate respect for them and their ideas. Schaffer (2019), the managing partner and co-founder of CSuite Solutions, a national healthcare advisory firm, believes listening is just the beginning for leaders. They must let their teams know that their ideas matter and that their decisions affect the business. If leaders ask for feedback but don't use it, people will feel like their ideas don't matter and will stop giving input. This can help you build successful relationships with your team.

Listening, genuinely listening, goes hand in hand with observation. It is about more than just hearing words; it is about making meaningful connections through eye contact, body language, and active engagement. By mastering this skill, I've fostered deeper connections with colleagues and gained valuable insights into their perspectives. Listening, as a soft skill, plays a crucial role in fostering organization and productivity. Just as staying organized through tools like calendars and apps is the foundation of efficiency, effective listening is the bedrock of meaningful communication. By attentively listening to instructions, feedback, and the needs of others, you streamline processes, reduce misunderstandings, and enhance your ability to stay on top of your responsibilities. In my own experience, I've found that combining good listening habits with strong organizational tools not only maximizes productivity but also ensures a smoother and more collaborative work environment

(Active) Listening as a Soft Skill.

As stated earlier, listening means making an intentional effort to pay attention to what someone says, and it is a crucial skill often missing in many organizations. You can listen in different ways, such as by making eye contact, nodding, and not interrupting.

Active listening involves focusing, understanding, and responding thoughtfully to what is being said. To *actively* listen, however, is to go further by being alert and appreciative. This means not being constructively critical or discriminative to the story presented to you. As an active listener, the goal is to learn and understand rather than criticize or judge. This approach fosters better communication, trust, and empathy between individuals, leading to more productive and harmonious relationships in both personal and professional settings.

Being an active listener is crucial in various facets of life, including professional environments. Active listening involves paying attention to details and encouraging open information sharing. One effective technique is setting a time limit, such as three minutes, for someone to share their story concisely. This approach helps maintain focus and respects everyone's time in a professional context, allowing for more efficient communication and understanding.

Try to avoid interrupting the narrator at all costs during that time. After actively listening, summarize and repeat what you heard and observe the body language of the narrator to give them an extra level of understanding. Use brief verbal statements like "I see," "I know," "Sure," "Thank you," or "I understand" to build trust and establish rapport. Demonstrate that you are committed to understanding the narrator's point of view through genuine nonverbal cues like nodding, eye contact, leaning forward, and paraphrasing to show understanding. The expression of these skills goes a long way in setting you apart from your colleagues.

Regarding (active) listening, expressing interest genuinely through nonverbal cues like body language is essential. You might be curious about people who pretend to pay attention, leading to awkward situations. Additionally, cultural norms regarding verbal and nonverbal cues vary, so it is worth considering how active listening differs across cultures. For instance, avoiding direct eye contact can signify respect in some cultures. These are just a few factors to remember and possibly address when exploring (active) listening.

Cooperation as a Soft Skill.

Think of cooperation as dealing with the results of a contested election. When the politician you support wins, you are excited. When the less preferred politician wins, you "accept" the results and hope for the best. You may not have to like the new politician, but you must respect the process that won them the election. To cooperate is to transfer information to team members with the least access to it. To cooperate means that you must understand collaboration and add the responsibilities of delegation, decision-making, accountability, and partial interdependence to all group members. Furthermore, cooperation requires fostering a supportive environment where team members actively listen to each other's perspectives and work together to achieve common goals.

In the professional world, cooperation is akin to navigating the aftermath of a contested election. Just as you celebrate when your preferred candidate wins, you must accept the outcome graciously when they don't, respecting the democratic process. Cooperation involves sharing information with team members who need it most and understanding the intricacies of collaboration, including delegation, decision-making, accountability, and partial interdependence. It is about fostering a supportive environment where everyone actively listens to each other's perspectives and collaborates to achieve shared objectives. This translates to the workplace, where cooperation is essential for successful teamwork and attaining common goals.

Collaboration as a Soft Skill.

The skill to collaborate – the process where more than two people or organizations work together to complete a task or achieve a goal – requires authentic leadership. It takes much willpower for some people to collaborate and cooperate to complete tasks. It involves respecting and valuing team or group members' skills, experiences, creativity, and contributions. As a result, specific guidelines for collaboration must be set for a team. Good managers must understand and embrace diversity, listen to and acknowledge the feelings, concerns, opinions, and ideas of others in the team or group, know each person in the team, encourage networking through strategic coalitions, and foster collective impact initiatives. More importantly, fostering a culture that acknowledges the challenge of discerning between various collaborative agendas and determining the most suitable for different situations is crucial.

Coordination as a Soft Skill.

Consider when you first learned how to drive and prepared to take the driver's license road test. Just like driving requires coordination between your hands, feet, and eyes to operate the vehicle smoothly, coordination in other contexts involves synchronizing different parts or aspects to work together effectively. Whether in sports, music, or even teamwork in the workplace, coordination is essential for achieving desired outcomes. It is about harmonizing efforts and actions to accomplish tasks efficiently and precisely.

The test required you to utilize all your cognitive abilities to operate the vehicle smoothly. You adjusted your seat for comfort and remained alert by paying close attention to your surroundings. You focused on ensuring the functionality of your car, including knowing turn signals, operating the windshield wipers, and avoiding obstacles like the bright orange cones. With your hands in the appropriate areas of the steering wheel and your feet on the necessary pedals for gas and brakes, each action contributed to the overall coordination required to maneuver a vehicle to pass the test effectively.

Like the driver's test, coordination extends beyond driving. Diverse teams need efficient collaboration toward a common goal to ensure team members move together in coordination with precision, speed, and purpose. It serves as a vital tool for fostering teamwork and facilitating the achievement of organizational objectives and matched efforts across teams while addressing issues that could arise from individual differences. For instance, in a new government setting, effective coordination involves multiple teams coordinating tasks through simultaneous actions and exchanging information systematically to maintain order and achieve desired outcomes. Mastering these subtle soft skills will enhance your coordination abilities.

Mediation as a Soft Skill.

Mediation in the workplace is when upset parties meet with a neutral, qualified HR manager to assist in resolving the issue. Mediation requires knowing when to and understanding how to intervene during a dispute. Without a doubt, this is a difficult task. Diplomats have tried to resolve issues on the world stage for generations that remain prevalent. You may ask yourself, "Why is this important to me?" Mediation is a soft skill, and when you attempt to master it, you will more likely be in the fast lane to promotions. For example, an HR manager may bring each party to the table to discuss the matter in a positive tone. From that discussion, the manager gathers information about the issue, identifies the unique nuances of the problems, sets the bargaining tools for negotiation, and applies a settlement medium desired by the parties. You can learn quickly from the process and extend the learning over time by monitoring how parties strive to sustain the settlement at the workplace.

Negotiation as a Soft Skill.

This soft skill is all about leading the charge to reach an agreement (in your favor). To do so, several factors must be hashed out before any deal is done, including the agreement for your manager to grant you the raise you desire. A prudent negotiator incorporates the best of all three. To use the aggressive approach does not mean to use a hostile attitude. Instead, it means to have an intentional/accidental mindset and to be verbally expressive (Schweinsberg, Thau, & Pillutla, 2022).

I want to talk about code-switching and its role in getting what you want in a negotiation. Code-switching is changing how you speak or act to fit different situations. I recommend practicing role-playing before your negotiation meetings. This helps you get comfortable with switching your language and behavior. Practicing this can make you more confident and prepared for the real thing.

If you have ever engaged in a constructive dialogue to resolve an issue, you likely have negotiated or compromised before, favorably or otherwise. A negotiation is an intentional discussion that settles a problem in a way that satisfies each party. In the negotiation process, each party endeavors to influence the other's perspective or stance to align with their views or objectives. By negotiating, all involved parties attempt to avoid arguing but agree to reach some form of compromise.

Negotiations happen more often than you can imagine. Most of the time, they occur informally at work, from allowing a colleague to stand in line in front of you at the cafeteria to taking the hourly shift of an associate or colleague. Successful negotiation requires following key collaborative steps. For example, take the need for a salary increase. You must adequately prepare for the meeting with your supervisor by reflecting on how you will negotiate getting a raise. Preparation requires you to have up-to-date information relevant to exchange with your supervisor to justify the raise. There are no shortcuts here. Bargaining is crucial. In other words, set a salary range that mirrors what the industry pays for similar or comparable positions you desire. Have a compelling argument that will secure the raise and execute from a winning standpoint.

The argument must be solidified by trust. Be ready to take a hard stand using your best communication skills while being responsible for the actions that come with the negotiation process. If you are still trying to get what you wanted or expected, understand that it is part of the process and learning experience. However, be prepared to present "another Plan A" rather than an alternate Plan B. You can propose a "segmented piecemeal plan" to your supervisor, which involves requesting small, incremental changes in specific areas that are important to you. This approach allows you to address your needs gradually, making it easier for you and your supervisor to find mutually beneficial solutions.

Adaptability as a Soft Skill.

Adaptability and flexibility are soft skills essential to embracing change. Both are particularly important when working in fast-paced or constantly changing work environments such as public relations, event management, nursing, and advertising. D. Allan

Boettger, senior director of corporate and community outreach at the University of Iowa's Pomerantz Career Center, meets with at least 100 companies a year to get an idea of the skills they seek in applicants. The basics like reliability, responsibility, good communication skills, and a can-do attitude remain on employers' "must" lists. Max McKeown's book, *Adaptability: The Art of Winning in An Age of Uncertainty*, lists adaptability as an integral human trait. The ability to adapt faster and smarter in any situation makes the influential difference between adapting to survive and adapting to win. The COVID pandemic has forced us to adapt to survive. Scoring an excellent interview opportunity leads to adapting to win. Human history is a story of adaptation and change. And, in this time of fierce competition, fear of human loss due to viral complications, and economic uncertainty, it has never been more crucial to understand how to adapt in new ways successfully. McKeown examines how stakeholders can improve their adaptability to gain advantageous positions through strict guidelines (McKeown, 2012).

Curiosity as a Soft Skill.

Curiosity, the desire to know or learn something new, is one skill I am thankful for mastering because I succeeded as an accomplished professional. In many African communities and elsewhere, people, especially children, who exhibit nosy, peculiar, and eccentric characteristics are frowned upon. However, curiosity offers people the power to endure uncertain circumstances and to ask tough questions, allowing them to win more chances afforded them while continuously seeking different ways to improve. For example, some of the most successful sales professionals demonstrate boundless curiosity. As a result, many organizations searching for new hires pay rapt attention to applicants who exhibit traits of curiosity.

Memory, insight, recall—these tools sharpen our edge in a competitive world. By exercising these faculties regularly, I've been able to stay agile and adaptable in the face of change. Questioning is the catalyst for innovation.

Self-management as a Soft Skill.

Self-management skills increase employee productivity. Critical examples of self-management skills are problem-solving, stress management, effective communication, and time management. It takes practice to become proficient in self-management skills. Earning a good GPA and obtaining a college degree requires self-management skills to the ultimate level.

At the workplace, self-management skills help you sustain a better work environment among associates. This soft skill enhances resilience, patience, perceptiveness, self-confidence, persistence, and emotional regulation, providing a clear pathway to the reduction of costs, a focus on business outcomes, and resolving internal conflicts. Self-management skills can also identify weaknesses in other skills while allowing you to retain business knowledge and manage flexible demand-driven roles.

Decision-making as a Soft Skill.

Competency of soft skills leads to good decision-making for desired outcomes. Decision-making requires you to define a problem, challenge, or opportunity. After clearly explaining the issue, you must tap into the skills to entertain various possible solutions to evaluate the benefits and costs or pros and cons associated with all options. The most essential part of decision-making is making the decision.

Making decisions requires confidence to uphold selected responses. Understand that your peers and supervisor will judge you on how well you manage responsibilities and make decisions. Ultimately, you will be assessed by how you implement solutions. Delegation is essential here. The right people for the right tasks are the clarion call.

Patience as a Soft Skill.

A calm professional can use all their intellect or "know-how" to observe people and situations in a way that may be envious to many. Generally, people need to be patient. The need for more patience interrupts the selection of the appropriate types of tools to judge situations. Patient people are calm enough to ask questions rather than assume the reason behind behaviors and conditions. Patient people often maintain inner peace and wisdom. They have a plan and are more focused when achieving goals. Remaining calm can be challenging, especially under stress.

In a competitive workplace, remaining calm in any situation is an integral soft skill, but challenging. One way to keep calm is to use a journal or recording device to chronicle and process your feelings and thoughts. Get creative with choosing positive perceptions whenever in a non-calm situation. Furthermore, stay aware of your environment and the factors influencing your emotions. Opt to release or relinquish control over things that are beyond your control. Prioritize getting sufficient sleep, aiming for more than 7 hours whenever possible. Practice deep breathing techniques to manage stress effectively. Enjoy nature by just being outdoors. Exercise more in different ways that excite you. Embrace music by listening to your favorite artists and new music. Again, breathe ...

Optimism as a Soft Skill.

Optimism plays a vital role in effective management. It embodies a hopeful and confident outlook regarding future possibilities and the success of various outcomes. In the workplace, managers must maintain a belief in the positive results of their decisions, even when circumstances do not unfold as expected.

Consider a common scenario that illustrates optimism in action: an employee is navigating the exciting yet stressful process of buying a home. Amid a particularly challenging day at work, this individual remains hopeful that conditions will improve. Then, a notification from the bank arrives, confirming qualification for a home loan with an affordable interest rate. Although this employee may not have secured their dream home, they find an alternative option in a desirable neighborhood. This ability to focus on positive developments, even in the face of setbacks, exemplifies how optimism can influence both personal and professional situations.

Here are six strategies that can help you develop and enhance your optimism as a key soft skill.

First, try to look at life from a positive point of view. It can be helpful during times of uncertainty.

Second, take note of the company you keep at work and in your personal life. Ensure those around you are smarter in areas you lack, as this helps you learn and grow from their expertise, ultimately boosting your confidence and problem-solving abilities.

Third, turn off news that constantly offers unwelcome stories. It is easier than you think. We have access to all types of information through our electronic devices. However, we must pay attention to information that may be discouraging.

Fourth, write in a journal for a few minutes each day. If journal writing is not your thing, record your story on your electronic device.

Fifth, acknowledge what you cannot control within your power and focus your energy on what you can change.

And sixth, remember to accept the negative, no matter how bad. Acceptance paves the way for a proper healing process.

Open-mindedness as a Soft Skill.

Like curiosity, being open-minded is a soft skill that progressive companies crave. It is the willingness to consider and be open to receiving new ideas. Open-mindedness suggests having the capacity to consider other perspectives while exhibiting empathy or sympathy to different people, even when you disagree with them. Because we live in a diverse world where we engage and work with people from across the globe, being open-minded fosters better collaboration, understanding, and innovation in the workplace.

Kendra Cherry, an author, educational consultant, and speaker, focuses on helping students learn about psychology. In her online publication, *The Benefits of Being Open-Minded*, Cherry explains that you can better understand yourself, the world, and the people around you when you are open-minded. You challenge yourself to absorb new ideas that require mental strength that is beneficial in the workplace. When you maintain an open mind, you actively absorb new ideas, which requires mental strength that is highly advantageous in the workplace (Cherry, 2023; Taylor, 2016). This mindset is crucial as it promotes innovation, creativity, and adaptability among teams. It enables individuals to welcome diverse perspectives, think critically about fresh concepts, and collaborate effectively with colleagues. Such openness fosters a positive work environment where teams can explore multiple solutions to challenges, enhancing decision-making and overall organizational advancement.

Creativity is a broad type of open-minded soft skill that can help you develop innovative solutions to problems at work. Instructional designers, architects, and artists are examples of careers where creativity is crucial to success. In *11 Soft Skills, Healthcare Executives Need: What You Didn't Learn in School*, Nicholas Hamm cited Jennifer Carney, vice president of finance and analytics at Beth Israel Deaconess Care Organization, who emphasized creativity and adaptability as essential for solving modern medical care problems (Hamm, 2019). It can also help you stand out and make you more attractive to employers. Creativity can help you make a name for yourself and give you an edge in the job market. For example, a creative approach in healthcare might involve designing patient-centered care initiatives that improve outcomes while reducing costs, showcasing your ability to innovate in a critical field.

Self-confidence as a Soft Skill.

In their article, *Measuring Self-Confidence in Workplace Settings: A Conceptual and Methodological Review of Measures of Self-Confidence, Self-Efficacy, and Self-Esteem*, Kane et al. (2021) discuss the importance of self-confidence in professional environments. They introduce the Embodied, Dynamic, and Inclusive (EDI) model, which emphasizes Authenticity, Competence, and Connectedness. This model illustrates how self-confidence influences performance, detailing the processes of losing and building confidence, and underscores the importance of maintaining the right mindset for success.

Self-confidence is an attitude reflecting your skills and abilities, requiring self-acceptance and trust to maintain control in life. Understanding your strengths and weaknesses enables you to set achievable goals, communicate assertively, and handle criticism constructively.

Self-confident individuals demonstrate gratitude, maintain regular exercise habits, foster positivity, and exhibit resilience in the face of challenges. They speak confidently, embrace risk-taking, learn from mistakes, support others, and prioritize active listening. Modesty and dedication to meaningful pursuits further characterize their approach. Possessing these traits aligns you with principles of professional success, positioning you positively in various workplace environments. It requires you to trust yourself enough to have control in your life. A self-confident person knows their strengths and weaknesses well to set realistic expectations and goals, communicate assertively, and handle criticism usefully.

When resumes land on their desks, many HR managers focus on knowledge, skills, abilities, and personalities (what many refer to as KSAP). During interviews, panelists look out for candidates who confidently answer questions. They are also attentive to how well candidates communicate their past experiences and handle unexpected questions. A confident candidate can set themselves apart by showing their ability to stay composed and think critically under pressure.

Organization Skills as a Soft Skill.

By a mile, organizational skills are one of the most important and transferable job skills an employee can acquire. Organized people embody a set of capabilities that help them plan, prioritize, and achieve their goals, which, in turn, can save a company time and money. Good organizational skills require you to efficiently manage time and resources, organize work assignments (workload), and schedule and prioritize projects. These factors help you improve your productivity and lower your stress level.

137

During a job interview, consider sharing your organizational strengths as a priority. When answering questions about the last organization you worked for, reflect on what you did to stay organized. Give specific examples of methods and tools you used, the impact on your work routine, and the benefits of your organization strategies to your previous company. To maintain this soft skill, make it a priority.

All interview questions should pass the organizational skills test. This means that every question should evaluate how well a candidate can manage tasks, prioritize responsibilities, and maintain efficiency in their work. Employers are looking for individuals who can demonstrate their ability to stay organized and handle multiple demands in a structured manner, which is crucial for success in any professional setting.

Self-motivation as a Soft Skill.

Self-motivation is the power that pushes you to keep going. It is a human internal drive to produce, develop, achieve, and keep moving forward. When you think you're ready to quit a task or don't know how to start an adventure, your self-motivation pushes you to go on. Americans moved on after some of the significant tragedies that beset us – 9/11, the Oklahoma City bombing, Pulse nightclub, and Sandy Hook Elementary School mass shootings – people who survived these events tapped into their self-motivation skills to move on by establishing The National September 11 Memorial & Museum; Oklahoma City National Memorial & Museum; Facebook's Safety Check feature in the Orlando, Florida area following the shooting by allowing Facebook users to mark themselves as safe to alert family and friends which set the tone as a first-of-its-kind feature in the United States; and renewed debate about gun control and effects of violent video games nationwide respectively. Self-motivation urges people to keep going despite setbacks, take up opportunities, and show responsibility for their goals.

Problem-solving as a Soft Skill.

Problem-solving abilities are a blend of analytical and creative thinking to find solutions. Careers where problem-solving is vital include law enforcement, information technology, and medical-related fields. Dennis Pierce, an education writer, explained in the Community College Journal, Employers across a wide variety of industries say the so-called "soft" skills such as problem-solving, critical thinking, communication, *and collaboration have grown in importance as rapid advancements in technology have transformed their operations* (Pierce, 2015, p. 23). A survey from the *National Association of Colleges and Employers* suggested that problem-solving and the ability to work well in a team are qualities employers desire the most from new hires (Gray, 2024). Yet, these are often the skills that employers struggle the most to fill. As these skills gradually increase in importance, employers look to community colleges to fill that gap, as these skills are essential.

Logical Reasoning as a Soft Skill.

Persuasive speakers rely on four logical ways of thinking to understand the line of reasoning: deductive, inductive, causal, and analogical. First, deductive reasoning is like planning ideas aimed at the highest output from spending from a budget. Second, inductive reasoning is a new learning process based on how users interact with the software. Third, for causal reasoning, an example is increased sick leave of staff due to getting sick resulting from not wearing facial covering at the workplace. Fourth, analogical reasoning assesses relationships between different occurrences of situations.

Applicant A, a qualified male applicant with locks, walks through the door for an interview. Applicant B, the next qualified applicant wearing a short-sleeved shirt, walks through the door with tattoos emblazoned on both arms for a scheduled job interview. Because both applicants share personal attributes that are not typical of your working environment, an assertion is made that Applicant A is likely to wear a tattoo as well. The above argument is deductive but not informative about what is important – whether they are appropriately qualified for the job regardless of their attributes! Be on the lookout for these logical reasoning traits so as not to distract you from what is important when placed in a leadership position.

Logical reasoning is the compass that guides decision-making. By gathering and analyzing information from diverse sources, I've been able to approach situations with clarity and foresight. It is about viewing challenges from multiple angles and finding innovative solutions that drive progress. Introspection is the key to personal growth. Taking the time to reflect on past experiences allows us to learn and evolve. I've found that by embracing introspection, I've been able to identify areas for improvement and chart a course toward self-improvement.

Persistence as a Soft Skill.

According to psychiatrist and geneticist Dr. C. Robert Cloninger, who holds the Wallace Renard Professorship of Psychiatry at Washington University in St. Louis, Missouri, persistence is a significant trait in psychology. He is renowned for his expertise in personality traits and played a crucial role in developing the *Temperament and Character Inventory*, which scientifically measures persistence, among other characteristics (Cloninger et al., 1994).

Alongside harm avoidance, novelty seeking, and reward dependence, persistence is one of the four temperament traits that shape an individual's identity. Think of persistence as determination taken to the next level. It refers to maintaining a steadfast course of action despite challenges such as fatigue, obstacles, or opposition. Persistence often leads to success. Achieving your current degree undoubtedly requires persistence, and the same level of determination will be essential for success in the workplace.

143

Employers value employees who demonstrate grit and resilience, especially during challenging times like the COVID-19 pandemic. Displaying your persistence during job interviews can significantly enhance your chances of securing your desired position with a forward-thinking organization.

Observation as a Soft Skill.

Specifically, I am talking about *qualitative* observation here. As a leader in your work group, the skill to measure and monitor two of the five sensory organs – hearing and sight – and their functioning and characteristics are fundamental. This activity may be subjective, but it calls for the attention of members of a team to discuss nuances that crop up before they escalate into unwanted scenarios. The natural ability to notice and stop conversations that could start rumors is not taught in college or at work. If you have or develop this skill, you will quickly move up in your career. This skill helps maintain a positive work environment and prevents misunderstandings. You become an asset to your organization by managing workplace communication effectively.

Persuasion as a Soft Skill.

Persuasion is one of the most essential skills to have at all costs! If you have ever convinced a loved one – a parent, for example – to get what you want, you are in a good lead. As you may know, many kids cry at the top of their lungs to get what they want from their parents. I am not asking you to cry here; I am far from it.

But I am asking that you learn the skill of telling your story in compelling ways to get ahead that can be useful when you desire a raise, want your team to buy into your idea, or lobby for your department to get additional resources in the budget. The art of persuasion is a leadership skill that requires the use of combined soft skills to set you apart from others to get what you need.

Brainstorming as a Soft Skill.

This skill can be tricky for introverted professionals who prefer to avoid working in groups. What has worked for me is my belief that wisdom lies not with a single person (at the workplace). As a result, I prefer to solve organizational challenges with other members and problem-solve challenges using techniques that involve the spontaneous contribution of ideas from all group members. Brainstorming may be conducted over several brainstorming sessions for members in small groups and cohort learning, mulling over ideas by one or more persons to devise or find a solution to organizational problems. Working with other low-ranking professionals for new and helpful ideas is okay.

Matthew Lynch, a staff writer with *The Tech Edvocate*, cites four types of brainstorming options – reverse, stop-and-go, Phillips 66, and brainstorming – for use by professionals at the workplace (Lynch, 2023). In reverse brainstorming, problems are reviewed using unorthodox, new, and different ways to generate new insights. Stop-and-go brainstorming technique requires that group members share unreviewed ideas by group members in short meeting sessions. You may be familiar with this process if you have any experience in peer learning exercises. For Phillip 66 brainstorming, six people suggest new ideas for six uninterrupted minutes. Then, a spokesperson for each group shares the best ideas with the larger group. Finally, the brainwriting option is where individual members of a group detail their thoughts in their preferred documented mediums (journals, memos, recorded audio, etc.) and share them with their group members for further consideration (De Garrido, Gómez Sanz & Pavón Mestras, 2021). In a world that is volatile, uncertain, complex, and ambiguous (VUCA), professionals must work collaboratively on all levels to achieve the maximum impact desired. It is even more necessary that you attain all skills in these areas to compete fairly and responsibly.

Work Ethic as a Soft Skill.

Work ethic reveals the relevance of work and determines the importance of work and its ability to improve the character of workers. Demonstrating a work ethic should be necessary in every career, but it is vital for first responders, teachers, and nurses. It advocates for personal accountability and responsibility.

As a college graduate, I understand how important work ethic is to your career success. Many managers still believe that employees must have a strong work ethic - they must work hard, be responsible, and be diligent. These managers think that many employees today are not as willing to work hard now to get rewards later. This was a vital part of the early Protestant work ethic in the United States. These managers' concerns are like what some writers have predicted about our society. For example, the influence of how people are raised, the emphasis on wanting things instantly, and the pressure from technology to work anywhere and anytime.

Porter (2005) states that there is pressure on both individuals and organizations to work hard. However, the organizational side of this has been looked at by seeing the negative results of specific policies and practices. Managers still expect employees to have a strong work ethic, but many believe that modern attitudes and pressures have led to a decline. Research suggests that maintaining a good work ethic is still vital for having a successful career. Employers continue to prize candidates who understand the culture of work. It is important to show up on time, be prepared, and take initiative to get ahead. A good work ethic means you are dependable and capable, making you more attractive to employers. It also means you will put in extra effort to reach your goals. Building a strong work ethic now will help you succeed in your career for years to come.

Since 2024, members of the Baby Boomer generation have dominated the American workforce in terms of power, influence, and control over institutional structure. They consider hard work and the Protestant Work Ethic (PWE) responsible for economic successes seen in America and Europe during the turn of the twentieth century. As a college graduate, you should know the importance of a strong work ethic. PWE is an integral part of that. It is a set of values emphasizing hard work, discipline, and dedication to achieving your goals. It is all about putting in the effort and not giving up when things get tough. This attitude will help you stand out in the job market and show employers that you are serious about succeeding, too. Miller, Woehr, and Hudspeth (2002) wrote a profound article on this topic. According to this article, people with high PWE places work central to their lives, avoids wasting time, and is ethical in their dealings with others. So, remember always to stay focused and dedicated to your goals, and the PWE will be a great asset to your career success.

Millennials have been seen as idle, arrogant, faithless, disrespectful, and requiring steady help. However, Kadakia — who is herself a Millennial, organizational development consultant, and a two-time TEDx speaker — displays that not only are these negative ideas wrong, but each one masks a beneficial work practice that progressive firms must accept if they plan to last (Kadakia, 2017). She states how the appearance of digital technology is the significant basis of many Millennial behaviors and gives a handbook, *The Millennial Myth: Transforming Misunderstanding into Workplace Breakthroughs*, for what our classic workplace must do to draw in, engage, and keep up-to-date personnel.

Vulnerability as a Soft Skill.

Vulnerability is an integral part of success throughout life. According to Brené Brown, author of the book *Daring Greatly: How the Courage to Be Vulnerable Transforms the Way We Live, Love, Parent, and Lead*, vulnerability is essential to building relationships and success in your career. According to Brown (2015), when we are open and honest, it allows us to have meaningful conversations, build trust, and create authentic relationships with others. This helps us succeed in whatever we do, whether leading a team, getting a job promotion, or making meaningful connections in a field. College graduates must be open to learning, growing, and taking risks to reach goals.

Margaret Cary, CEO of The Cary Group Global, a leadership coaching organization, also believes that vulnerability with employees is key. Vulnerability is being transparent and being present, which means communicating your feelings and understanding the feelings of others (Cary, 2017). When you're vulnerable in the workplace, it encourages trust between you and your employees, which leads to stronger relationships and better communication. Being open and vulnerable in the workplace can also help you receive feedback from your team, which is essential for career success. So, being vulnerable is an important skill if you're a college graduate and want to succeed in your career.

Time Management Skills as a Soft Skill.

Time management is critical to success in your career as a college graduate. Learning to plan, prioritize, and organize your tasks effectively is essential so you can make the most of your time. According to Morgenstern (2004), successful time management can help you finish more quickly while avoiding burnout and stress. Similarly, Brian Tracy's book *Eat That Frog!* explains that tackling your most demanding tasks can reduce procrastination and increase productivity (Tracy, 2017). Managing your time will help you be more successful in your career.

A significant plus is showing your supervisor you can get stuff done quickly and efficiently by using your time effectively. This is especially true if you're in IT project management, loss prevention, or a legal job. Employers have been preparing for the arrival of members of Generation Z – people born between 1997 and 2013 – for some time now. Managers need to understand the unique traits of Gen Z and how they differ from Millennials. That way, they can better integrate the new employees and help them find success. Authors like Stemmle (2019) and Palmer (2018) have written about the importance of time management and how it can help college grads find career success.

Schroth (2019) discusses how managers must adjust to the needs of the newest generation in the workforce, Generation Z. This group differs from previous generations in that they are more independent, focused on their career goals, and have a stronger sense of social responsibility and activism. If you are a Gen Z graduate, you can cope with the unique characteristics of your generation by embracing technology for productivity, staying adaptable in a rapidly changing job market, and leveraging your digital skills to network and find new opportunities. You can take advantage of the technology available and use it to your advantage. You can also focus on career development and be open to feedback and new ideas. Additionally, you can create a culture of inclusion in your workplace and be socially responsible. By taking these steps, you can be better prepared for the workplace and set yourself up for career success.

By challenging assumptions and seeking out new perspectives, I've been able to push the boundaries of what's possible and drive meaningful change. Time management is the bridge between ambition and achievement. By setting clear goals, prioritizing tasks, and managing my schedule effectively, I've been able to strike a balance between work and leisure, ensuring sustained success in the long run.

Leadership as a Soft Skill.

Being a leader is a significant part of having a successful career after college. Leadership allows you to control and guide others to help you reach your organization's goals. Many people nowadays are part of the Millennial Generation, which means employers are facing some of the biggest challenges ever. Millennials are hard-working and achievement-oriented but sometimes need help in the leadership and problem-solving departments. Books written by Howe and Strauss (2000) and Rainer Thom and Rainer Jess (2011) help us learn more about this generation and how to help them become successful leaders.

Leadership is an essential skill allowing you to direct others while achieving your organization's goals. This is especially important for entrepreneurs, managers, and teachers. The first group of Millennials – people born between 1980 and 2001 – are now entering the workforce, and employers are facing challenges yet to be experienced. Millennials are a large group, with 92 million compared to the 78 million Baby Boomers (Fisherman, 2016). As such, they are the pride and joy of their parents, and they have a lot of demands and expectations. Although Millennials work hard and are goal-oriented, they don't always have the skills for leadership and solving problems. They want the freedom and flexibility of a virtual office, but they need clear instructions.

Authors like Schawbel (2018) and Pollak (2019) explain how to understand Millennials and how companies can adjust to recruit them. Alsop (2008) provides insight into this generation and how companies adapt to recruiting. It explains why Millennials are drawn to specific jobs, how they differ from past generations, and what they need to succeed.

Attention to Detail as a Soft Skill.

As a recent college grad, paying attention to details is a must if you want to succeed in the professional world. Careers suited to detail-oriented people include accounting, pharmacology, and engineering. Attention to detail is the ability to achieve thoroughness and accuracy when accomplishing a task. That means making sure all your work is accurate and that you are always double-checking it. Even the most minor mistakes can make a huge difference. Murphy (2015) stresses that attention to detail is crucial for success. Robert Half, CEO of Robert Half International, emphasized that attention to detail is a crucial skill for job seekers aiming to stand out and excel (Half, 2024).

Attention to detail allows you to be thorough and accurate in your work. By 2030, Deloitte Global and the Global Business Coalition for Education believe that more than half of the nearly two billion young people worldwide won't possess the abilities or educational background necessary to get a job (Global, 2018). They suggest that recent graduates should have the skills needed to successfully compete in the workforce, including but not limited to learning how to use technology, being straightforward and clear, and having a flexible plan for making decisions.

Digital Mindset as a Soft Skill.

Australian professors Bacalja, Beavis, and O'Brien (2022) examined how educational practices regarding digital literacy are viewed from various perspectives in Australia and how these differing viewpoints shape our experiences in the digital era. Their research highlighted the crucial role of creativity in facilitating digital learning. As recent graduates, we must equip ourselves for life in the digital realm. This entails grasping the implications of emerging technologies such as platformatization, artificial intelligence, edu-apps, and algorithms on our readiness for the workplace. For example, platformatization refers to the process by which digital platforms, such as social media networks, online marketplaces, and other web-based services, become central intermediaries in various sectors, influencing how information, goods, services, and interactions are organized and managed. This concept highlights the growing power and influence of these platforms in shaping economic, social, and cultural activities.

It is not just about mastering the tools; it is about embracing a digital mindset where user needs are paramount, customization is key, and innovation is constant. While this may seem daunting, it is the necessary path to staying relevant.

Traditionally, workplaces have been structured around the preferences of a few select leaders. However, we must pivot towards designing workplaces prioritizing users' needs, including customers and employees. Cultivating a digital mindset is central for recent college graduates to thrive in their careers. It involves comprehending and adapting to the ever-evolving digital landscape, leveraging digital tools for communication and collaboration, and confidently utilizing them to achieve career aspirations.

Transparency as a Soft Skill.

In today's professional landscape, transparency is paramount. It is not just about being honest; it is about shedding light on the inner workings of your organization. This transparency fosters better decision-making by ensuring that everyone within the system is well-informed. Unfortunately, silos between departments often obscure what others are working on, and the actions of senior leadership remain shrouded in mystery. We must implement strategies to increase visibility into our business decisions across the organization to overcome this. By doing so, we empower individuals at all levels to make informed choices that drive success.

To thrive in your career, honesty and openness are non-negotiables. Transparency isn't just about providing information; it is about being forthright, offering accurate insights, and avoiding the temptation to conceal anything. For recent college graduates, maintaining transparency is essential for building trust with colleagues, supervisors, and future employers. Estlund (2010) and Kaputa (2016) noted that transparency cultivates trust between employers and employees, fostering heightened productivity and engagement. By embracing transparency, recent graduates can forge meaningful relationships with their employers and contribute to a more positive work environment.

Speed as a Soft Skill.

The world is moving faster than ever, yet our work processes are becoming more complex and cumbersome. Millennials simply cannot understand why it takes us so long to change, and at this point, neither should the other generations! We need to figure out how to move our decision-making more quickly to match the speed of what's happening around us. This adaptation is crucial to remaining competitive and responsive in today's dynamic environment.

As someone who's navigated through the twists and turns of a career, I've come to understand the value of soft skills in shaping success. In a world where change is the only constant, the ability to adapt and evolve is crucial. Millennials, with their penchant for speed and innovation, have forced us to reconsider our approach to decision-making. We shed our reluctance and embrace agility to keep pace with the rapidly shifting landscape.

Effective decision-making hinges on sharp observation skills, which are indispensable in today's fast-paced workplace. Whether swiftly navigating through tasks or strategically probing with precise inquiries, honing this skill reveals deeper insights crucial for staying ahead. Authors like Litalien (2012) and Notter and Grant (2012) underscore the critical role of keen observation in deciphering the intricacies of contemporary work environments, where rapid adaptation and acute awareness are paramount for success.

Soft skills are often overlooked but are crucial in achieving career success. Developing these skills improves our abilities and positively impacts our organization. Let's recognize the importance of soft skills and work together to build a more promising future.

The Importance of Soft Skills

Throughout my career, I've learned firsthand the undeniable importance of soft skills. Dr. Jessy John explained in his article that soft skills training programs influence the development of soft skills among management students (John, 2009). According to his study, a staggering 85 percent of success can be attributed to these invaluable skills. It is not just about technical prowess. It is about the intangible qualities that set us apart in a competitive landscape.

Wats and Wats (2009) delve into the evolving education and employment landscape. As educational paths diversify and the job market grows increasingly competitive, students must augment their hard and soft skills to distinguish themselves. While hard skills encompass academic prowess and expertise, soft skills encompass interpersonal, communication, and adaptability abilities. Research suggests that while hard skills contribute to a mere 15% of success, soft skills constitute a substantial 85%. Employers seek individuals who exhibit dependability, integrity, effective communication, and a willingness to learn (Deepa & Seth, 2013; Lyu & Liu, 2021).

As per Roepe (2017), 94% of recruiters assert that exceptional soft skills hold more weight than experience when promoting individuals to leadership roles. These skills aren't just necessary for landing your dream job today but are also crucial for advancing your career. With the continuous expansion of automation, soft skills are poised to become even more critical in setting candidates apart in the eyes of employers. So, honing your interpersonal, communication, and adaptability abilities isn't just a good idea—it is essential for navigating the evolving job market and securing future opportunities for professional growth.

Lisa Rabasca Roepe (2017) highlights the importance of soft skills in career advancement. She cites Forbes' findings, indicating that 94% of recruiters prioritize top-notch soft skills - problem-solving, oral communication, and adaptability - over experience when considering promotions to leadership positions. These skills aren't just essential for securing desired positions in the present but indispensable for navigating career growth. Moreover, as automation continues to expand, Roepe emphasizes that soft skills will emerge as even more significant differentiators in the eyes of employers. Therefore, investing in developing interpersonal, communication, and adaptability abilities isn't merely advantageous—it is imperative for thriving in today's dynamic job market and securing future opportunities for professional advancement. Reflecting on my path, I realize that my ability to communicate effectively, collaborate seamlessly, and adapt to changing circumstances has been instrumental in my professional growth.

Susan Vitale, Chief Marketing Officer of Internet Collaborative Information Management Systems (iCIMS), succinctly captures the essence of soft skills by explaining that while hard skills may grab attention, soft skills make us stand out and secure the job (iCIMS,

2017). I've seen this play out time and again in various industries. Soft skills are the linchpin of success, whether its mechanics relying on active listening and feedback to troubleshoot issues or healthcare providers leveraging their empathy and communication skills to connect with patients.

As automation continues to reshape the workplace, the value of soft skills will only intensify. In a world where technology can handle the technical aspects, human touch—our ability to empathize, collaborate, and innovate — sets us apart. I've internalized this lesson over the years. It has driven me to continuously hone my soft skills and stay ahead of the curve. So, as you embark on your career journey, remember that while technical skills are essential, soft skills propel you forward. Take the time to cultivate these qualities and watch as doors of opportunity swing open before you.

Your journey through soft skills has been nothing short of transformative. Through introspection, learning, and practice, you understand that while technical expertise may open doors, mastering soft skills propels you forward in your career. Peggy Klaus's timeless wisdom serves as a guiding beacon, reminding you that soft skills are not just an afterthought but the very essence of professional success. As you stand at the threshold of the future, carry with you a newfound appreciation for communication, emotional intelligence, adaptability, and teamwork — all vital components of navigating the complexities of the modern workplace.

Armed with this knowledge, you are ready to embrace the challenges and opportunities that lie ahead, confident in your ability to navigate the dynamic landscape of the professional world. With each interaction, each decision, and each endeavor, continue to cultivate and hone your soft skills, recognizing them not only as tools for career advancement but as pillars of personal growth and fulfillment. Do so with gratitude for the lessons learned and excitement for the possibilities that await, knowing that with a strong foundation in soft skills, you are well-equipped to thrive in whatever the future may hold.

CHAPTER 4

How do I look?

"If you are feeling good, you look good, you are confident about yourself, you are going to go out there, and you will rock it" (Jorgic, 2016).

Michelle Carter

Michelle Carter was an American shot putter and Olympic women's champion.

In the professional world, appearance often plays a significant role. However, it is also important to recognize that dressing well isn't just about meeting societal norms or impressing others. Dressing well can boost your confidence and professionalism, helping you feel more prepared and capable in various situations. It is about presenting yourself in a way that aligns with your values and respects your context. Ultimately, your attire can influence how you perceive yourself and others, contributing to your overall presence and impact.

World-class athlete Michelle Carter said it best, "*If you are feeling good, you look good, you are confident about yourself, you are going to go out there, and you will rock it*" (Jorgic, 2016). This chapter explores the importance of self-confidence and personal presentation in your professional journey, offering insights into how your appearance can influence your success.

Understanding the Power of Confidence

Let me share a little secret: confidence is your most outstanding accessory. In my journey through the professional world, I've realized that when you feel good about yourself, it radiates through every aspect of your being. It is not just about the clothes you wear or how you style your hair—it is about owning who you are with unshakable confidence. When you walk into a room with your head held high and a smile, people can't help but take notice.

Let me take you back to the most momentous of my career experience. I was preparing for a high-stakes presentation, feeling the weight of expectations bearing down on me. However, instead of succumbing to nerves, I consciously decided to channel my inner confidence. I reminded myself of all the hard work and preparation I had put into this moment and refused to let self-doubt hold me back. As I stepped onto the stage, I held my head high, greeted the audience with a genuine smile, and delivered my presentation with unwavering conviction. And you know what? It paid off. Not only did I receive positive feedback from my colleagues and superiors, but I also felt a sense of empowerment that carried me through future challenges.

Feeling confident isn't always easy, though. We all have self-doubt and insecurity, but how we overcome those moments genuinely defines us. Building confidence has been a gradual process of self-discovery and self-acceptance. It is about recognizing my strengths and embracing my flaws, knowing that they all contribute to the unique individual that I am. So, my advice to you is simple: believe in yourself, embrace your uniqueness, and let your confidence shine bright.

But confidence isn't just a state of mind—it is also a skill that can be cultivated and honed over time. One way to boost your confidence is by setting yourself up for success. Whether preparing thoroughly for a presentation or dressing in an outfit that makes you feel unstoppable, taking proactive steps to bolster your self-assurance can make all the difference. Surround yourself with supportive people who lift you and encourage you to be the best version of yourself.

Confidence isn't something that magically appears overnight—it is a mindset that requires cultivation and practice. One of the most effective ways to boost your confidence is by celebrating your strengths and accomplishments. Take stock of all your achievements, no matter how big or small, and allow yourself to bask in the glow of your success. Surround yourself with supportive friends, family members, and mentors who believe in your abilities and encourage you to reach for the stars. And remember, confidence is contagious. When you exude self-assurance and positivity, others can't help but be drawn to your magnetic energy. When you exude confidence, you inspire those around you to believe in themselves. So, don't be afraid to share your light with the world and empower others to do the same.

Of course, building confidence isn't just about puffing out your chest and pretending to be someone you're not. It is about embracing your true self—flaws and all—and recognizing that you are worthy of success and happiness just as you are. So, don't be afraid to let your authentic self-shine in every aspect of your life, from how you dress to how you interact with others. Embrace your unique quirks and imperfections and use them to your advantage. After all, it is our differences that make us exciting and memorable.

You'll encounter moments of doubt and uncertainty as you navigate your professional journey. But instead of allowing fear to hold you back, use it as an opportunity to push yourself out of your comfort zone and grow. Take on new challenges enthusiastically, knowing that overcoming each obstacle will only strengthen your confidence and resilience. And remember, confidence is a journey, not a destination. It requires constant nurturing and attention, so make it a priority. Believe in yourself, stay true to your values, and never underestimate the power of confidence to propel you toward your dreams.

Making First Impressions: Dressing for Success.

Picture this: You're standing in front of your closet, deciding what to wear for that crucial meeting or job interview. The truth is that your choice of attire speaks volumes before you even utter a word. Dressing for success isn't just about wearing the latest fashion trends or the most expensive designer labels—it is about dressing with purpose and intention. Find clothing that fits well, flatters your body type, and reflects your personal and professional style. Remember, when you look good, you feel good. And that confidence will carry you through any professional setting.

When it comes to dressing for success, it is essential to consider the context of the situation. What may be appropriate attire for a creative industry may not be in a more traditional corporate environment. Take cues from industry standards and your colleagues to ensure that your attire aligns with the expectations of your workplace. And don't forget the little details—like grooming and accessories—which can elevate your look and leave a lasting impression on others. By paying attention to these small but significant elements, you'll demonstrate your professionalism from a physical and aesthetic standpoint.

Start by understanding your workplace's dress code or the event you'll be attending. Is it formal, business casual, or something in between? Once you know the expectations, you can tailor your outfit accordingly. Remember, it is always better to be slightly overdressed than underdressed, as it shows respect for the occasion and the people you'll be interacting with.

When it comes to business casual dressing for college seniors and job seekers, it is all about striking the right balance between professionalism and comfort. I learned this firsthand when I entered the workforce with other professionals. I knew a button-down shirt or blouse paired with dress pants or a skirt could convey a polished yet approachable look. Adding a blazer or cardigan can add an extra touch of sophistication. It is important to remember that while dressing professionally or for success is essential, showcasing your comfort and confidence in your skin through your style is equally important in making a lasting impression (Black & van den Broek, 2013).

If you're not comfortable with what you're wearing, it will show in your body language and demeanor, undermining the impression you're trying to make. So, choose clothing that makes you feel powerful and poised, whether a tailored suit or a stylish dress and heels. And remember, confidence is the best accessory you can wear, so wear it proudly.

Dressing for success isn't merely about following the rules but expressing your style and personality. Your clothes are a form of self-expression, so don't be afraid to let your individuality shine. Find ways to infuse your personality into your wardrobe, whether it is a pop of color, a statement accessory, or a signature piece that reflects your unique taste.

Looking the part is only half the battle. Grooming and personal hygiene are equally important aspects of your overall appearance. Pay attention to details like neat hair, trimmed nails, and clean, wrinkle-free clothing. These may seem small, but they can make a big difference in how others perceive you. As you embark on your professional journey, don't be afraid to experiment with your style, and push traditional norms' boundaries.

To start, let's address the basics: personal care and hygiene. While it may seem trivial, these aspects can significantly affect how we are perceived in the workplace. Every detail counts, from using hand sanitizer to keep germs at bay to applying hand lotion for smooth and professional handshakes. And let's not forget about mints for fresh breath – a small gesture that can make a big difference in our interactions with colleagues. Now, for offensive hygiene, let's just say nobody wants to be known as the person with the overpowering armpit scent. So, let's be mindful of our grooming habits and take steps to ensure we're not causing any olfactory disturbances in the workplace!

Moving on, it is essential to acknowledge that personal care and hygiene conversations can sometimes be uncomfortable. However, they're necessary for maintaining a respectful and productive work environment. We can create a culture where everyone feels comfortable and valued by approaching these topics respectfully and compassionately. After all, when we care for ourselves, we're better equipped to contribute positively to the workplace and foster a culture of holistic innovation.

Ultimately, dressing for success is more than just making a good impression or looking good. It is about feeling confident and empowered in your skin. It is about projecting confidence, professionalism, and authenticity to the world. Take pride in your appearance, dress with purpose and intention, and watch as your outward image reflects the confident, capable professional you indeed are. So, choose clothing that makes you feel like the best version of yourself, and let your inner confidence radiate in every outfit you wear.

Body Language Matters.

Have you heard the saying, *Actions speak louder than words*? Regarding professional communication, your body language can tell a lot about you (Duffy & Feltovich, 2002). Every movement conveys a message to those around you, from your stance to your gestures. So, pay attention to your posture, maintain eye contact, and exude positivity through your facial expressions. When you project confidence and openness through your body language, you'll find that people are more receptive to your words.

It is not just about what you say but how you say it. In my experience, I've found that nonverbal cues can often speak volumes louder than words. For example, a firm handshake can convey strength and confidence, while avoiding eye contact may signal insecurity or disinterest. By mastering the art of body language, you can enhance your communication skills and forge stronger connections with colleagues, clients, and superiors.

Of course, body language isn't just about projecting confidence—it is also about being mindful of the messages you're sending to others. Take a moment to consider how those around you may perceive your posture, gestures, and facial expressions. Do you appear open and approachable, or closed-off and standoffish? By being aware of your body language and making subtle adjustments, you can ensure you send the right signals and foster positive interactions with others.

One of the keys to effective body language is good posture. Standing straight and tall makes you appear more confident, authoritative, and empowered.

Practice aligning your spine, relaxing your shoulders, and engaging your core muscles to maintain optimal posture throughout the day.

In addition to enhancing your communication skills, mastering body language can help you navigate challenging situations more effectively. For example, maintaining a calm and composed demeanor in high-pressure meetings or negotiations can convey authority and control, even in the face of adversity. By harnessing the power of body language, you can project confidence, build rapport, and ultimately achieve tremendous success in your professional endeavors.

Eye contact is another crucial aspect of body language (Kleinke, 1986). When you make eye contact with someone, you signal that you're engaged and attentive to what they're saying. It fosters a sense of connection and trust, which is essential for building strong professional relationships. Just be sure not to stare too intensely, as this can appear aggressive or intimidating.

Gestures can also convey a wealth of information about your thoughts and feelings. Use your hands to emphasize key points and add emphasis to your words but be mindful of excessive or distracting movements. Aim for natural and spontaneous gestures rather than forced or rehearsed. Finally, pay attention to your facial expressions, which can reveal much about your emotional state. A facial expression that lacks any sign of emotion (flat affect) can also signal negative non-verbal communication.

Practice projecting warmth and approachability through facial expressions to foster open and productive communication with those around you. For example, maintain a friendly smile and eye contact during conversations to convey attentiveness and openness. By mastering the art of body language, you can enhance your professional presence and make a lasting impact on those you encounter. Stand tall, make eye contact, and let your nonverbal cues speak volumes about your confidence, competence, and credibility. With some practice and mindfulness, you'll be amazed at its positive impact on your professional relationships and success. So, the next time you find yourself in a professional setting, remember the importance of body language in communication.

Understanding Cultural and Industry Norms.

While navigating different professional environments, I learned the importance of understanding and respecting cultural and industry norms. For example, acceptable behavior in one setting could be deemed inappropriate in another. Take the time to research and familiarize yourself with the expectations and standards of your particular industry and adapt your appearance accordingly as a form of respect for cultural diversity and industry traditions, demonstrating your professionalism and adaptability to colleagues and clients.

As you research, ask yourself: Is there a specific dress code or convention commonly followed in this industry? Are there any cultural or religious considerations that need to be considered? Cultural sensitivity isn't just about avoiding offensive behavior—it is also about actively embracing and celebrating diversity in all its forms. Take the time to learn about different cultural customs and traditions (Gupta et al., 2018). Whether greeting colleagues with a respectful bow or observing dietary restrictions during business meetings, small gestures of cultural awareness can go a long way toward building meaningful relationships and fostering a positive work environment.

Understanding cultural and industry norms is about recognizing and appreciating the values and customs of others. Whether working with colleagues from different cultural backgrounds or interacting with clients from around the world, it is essential to approach each interaction with sensitivity and empathy. You'll build stronger relationships and enrich your professional experience by embracing diversity and fostering an inclusive environment. For example, while a laid-back dress code might be the norm in the tech industry, a more formal dress code may be expected in finance or law. By aligning your appearance with industry standards, you'll demonstrate professionalism and respect for the traditions and expectations of your field.

Navigating cultural and industry norms can sometimes be challenging, especially in today's globalized world, where workplaces are increasingly diverse and interconnected. Understanding cultural and industry standards isn't just about following the rules—it is also about recognizing and challenging biases and stereotypes within your professional community. That's why it is crucial to approach each situation with an open mind and a willingness to learn. Don't be afraid to ask questions, seek feedback, and engage in conversations that broaden your understanding of cultural perspectives. By fostering a culture of respect and inclusivity, you'll create a more harmonious and productive work environment for everyone.

Take a proactive approach to promoting diversity and inclusion in your workplace, and advocate for change where necessary. By fostering a culture of respect, acceptance, and open-mindedness, you'll not only enhance your professional reputation. You will contribute to a more equitable and inclusive work environment for everyone. While navigating the complexities of cultural and industry norms in your professional journey, remember to approach each interaction with empathy, humility, and respect. By embracing diversity and understanding the unique perspectives of those around you, you will develop stronger relationships and succeed tremendously in your career. So, the next time you find yourself in a new professional setting, take a moment to observe and learn about the cultural and industry norms at play. As you value diversity, you enhance your professional reputation, contributing to an inclusive and equitable workplace for everyone.

The Impact of Personal Branding.

Your brand is your professional reputation. It sets you apart from the crowd and shapes how others perceive you. Every aspect of your appearance- how you dress and present yourself in person or online- contributes to your brand. So, take the time to curate a visual identity that aligns with your values and career aspirations. Whether crafting a polished professional social media profile or attending a networking event, let your brand radiate in every interaction.

When it comes to personal branding, authenticity is paramount. Don't try to be someone you're not or emulate the success of others—instead, focus on showcasing your unique strengths, talents, and personality. Reflect on these questions: What makes me stand out from the crowd? What are my passions, interests, and values? Like authenticity, consistency is essential in building a solid brand. Your appearance, communication style, and online presence should all reflect a cohesive image reinforcing your professional identity. Whether you're interacting with colleagues, clients, or potential employers, ensure that every touchpoint demonstrates your brand's values and attributes.

Later in this chapter, you can learn more about authenticity under the "Embracing Authenticity" sub-section. But personal branding isn't just about creating a polished image—it is also about authenticity and consistency. Your brand should reflect who you are and what you stand for. To make this connection, you must first identify your unique strengths, values, and passions, leveraging them to build a compelling and authentic narrative.

When constructing this narrative, start by defining your brand identity. What are your core values and beliefs? What are your professional goals and aspirations? Once you clearly understand who you are and what you want to achieve, you can shape your brand accordingly. Your appearance plays a significant role in shaping your brand. Whether you realize it or not, people judge you based on how you look, dress, and carry yourself. That's why you must be intentional about your visual presentation and ensure it aligns with your brand identity.

Personal branding is also essential to how you present yourself online in today's digital age. Your online presence is often the first impression that others have of you, so it is crucial to manage it carefully. From your professional social media profile to your personal social media posts, ensure your online persona is consistent with your brand and reinforces the professional image you want to project.

Take the time to authentically engage with your audience by sharing valuable insights on social media or offering support and mentorship. By positioning yourself as a trusted person and leader in your field, you'll attract opportunities and connections that align with your personal and professional goals. The time and effort you invest in building your brand will help distinguish you from your colleagues and position you as a leader in your field. So, take control of your professional narrative and let your brand radiate in every aspect of your in-person and online presence.

As you further develop and refine your brand, remember it is a journey, not a destination. Be open to feedback, adapt to changing circumstances, and continuously seek opportunities for growth and improvement while cultivating a positive reputation to ultimately leave a lasting legacy that inspires others to follow in your footsteps.

First impressions aren't just about how you look, act, or make others feel (Zebrowitz, 2004). Approach each interaction with warmth, authenticity, and genuine interest in the person you're meeting. Smile, ask questions, and listen attentively to what they say. You'll leave a lasting impression beyond surface-level appearances by showing empathy and building rapport. A first impression isn't just about projecting confidence and authenticity but about being mindful of unconscious and implicit biases and stereotypes that may influence others' perceptions of you. Take a proactive approach to challenging stereotypes and promoting diversity and inclusion across professional interactions.

Whether advocating for underrepresented voices in meetings or challenging outdated norms and practices, be an ally for change for a more inclusive work environment for everyone.

But what if you make a less-than-stellar first impression? Don't worry—we've all been there. The key is acknowledging missteps, learning from them, and striving to improve next time. Remember, every interaction is an opportunity to make a positive impression and build meaningful connections with others. So, put your best foot forward, be genuine, and let your authentic self-showcase itself in every encounter.

While navigating the complexities of the first impression in your professional journey, understand that authenticity is your greatest asset. Be true to yourself, embrace your unique strengths and qualities, and let your genuine personality radiate through every interaction. First impressions are more than just making a good impression; they are about building trust, fostering connections, and laying the foundation for productive relationships. With an authentic and positive first impression, doors to new opportunities will open, and strong relationships will be built within a more inclusive and supportive professional community.

Embracing Authenticity.

In a world where conformity often reigns supreme, there's incredible power in embracing your authenticity (Erickson, 1995). Your unique personality, quirks, and perspectives make you stand out in a sea of sameness.

But embracing authenticity isn't always easy, especially in professional settings where there may be pressure to conform to certain norms and expectations. It takes courage to be yourself unapologetically, but the rewards are worth it. When you embrace your authenticity, you attract opportunities and connections that align with your true self rather than trying to fit into someone else's mold.

One of the most potent ways to make a lasting impression is by showcasing your authenticity and genuine interest in others. Instead of focusing solely on promoting yourself or impressing others with your accomplishments, take the time to listen actively, ask thoughtful questions, and show empathy and understanding. You'll leave a memorable impression beyond surface-level interactions by demonstrating a genuine desire to connect and engage with those around you.

In steering through these waters, identify your core values, passions, and strengths. Once you have a clear sense of your authentic self, let it stand out in every aspect of your professional life. Whether it is speaking up for what you believe in, pursuing projects that ignite your passion, or expressing your style through your appearance, be true to yourself in all that you do.

Additionally, it is essential to recognize the importance of authenticity and transparency in building your social media presence (Erickson, 2021; Steils, Martin, & Toti, 2022). While it is tempting to embellish or exaggerate your accomplishments to impress potential employers or peers, honesty is paramount. Authenticity breeds trust and credibility, establishing a solid foundation for meaningful connections and opportunities. Be genuine in your interactions, openly share your successes and failures, and showcase the real person behind the professional facade. By staying true to yourself and your values, you'll attract like-minded individuals and foster genuine relationships that can support your career growth.

Embracing authenticity doesn't mean throwing professionalism out the window. It is about finding a balance between staying true to yourself and adhering to the expectations of your professional environment.

That may mean expressing your personality through subtle touches in your appearance, such as colorful accessories or playful patterns, while still dressing in a manner that's appropriate for the setting.

But perhaps most importantly, embracing authenticity is about owning your story and being proud of who you are. Your experiences, triumphs, and challenges have shaped you into the person you are today, and there's no shame in embracing your unique journey. So, stand tall, speak your truth, and let your authenticity guide your personal and professional life.

As you embark on your professional journey, remember that your appearance is more than just skin deep. It reflects your inner confidence, authenticity, and professionalism. By embracing the power of confidence and dressing with purpose and intention, you'll not only look the part but also feel empowered to take on any challenge that comes your way. Remember to pay attention to your body language, understand cultural and industry norms, and cultivate your brand with authenticity and consistency. And above all, never underestimate the impact of a positive first impression on your career. With these principles in mind, you'll not only look good—you'll exude the kind of confidence and presence that commands respect, opens doors, and paves the way for success.

CHAPTER 5

Successfully Navigating Social Media in the Digital Age

"We don't have a choice on whether we do social media, the question is how well we do it." Erik Qualman Quotes (n.d.).

Erik Qualman

Erik Qualman, author of *Socialnomics* (Qualman, 2022) and *Digital Leader* (Qualman, 2011), is a leading voice in social media's impact on life and business. He was named the 2nd Most Likeable Author after J.K. Rowling, author of the *Harry Potter* series.

In modern communication, *"We don't have a choice on whether we do social media. The question is how well we do it."* (Erik Qualman, n.d.). This quote is by Erik Qualman and teaches us that social media isn't just a choice or option anymore. It is a part of our lives, and how we use it can make a big difference. So, let's explore how social media and other forms of technology can help us succeed in school and beyond.

Understanding the Digital Landscape.

Imagine a world where everything is connected through technology, information travels fast, and we can instantly connect with people from around the globe. That's the digital landscape we live in today. Understanding this landscape is like having a map for navigation.

Digital communication has become ubiquitous in our modern world, shaping our interactions, influencing our decisions, and molding our perceptions. Technology permeates every aspect of our existence, from the palm of our hands to the screens surrounding us. It is essential to grasp the significance of this digital landscape, recognizing its power to connect individuals across vast distances, disseminate information instantaneously, and catalyze social change. As we embark on this exploration, let's delve deeper into the nuances of this digital ecosystem, navigating its complexities with curiosity and discernment.

Building Your Digital Presence.

Think of your online presence like your digital resume — it is how you present yourself to the world. Just like you want your resume to reflect your best self and impress future employers, your online presence should also accomplish those goals by presenting your interests, accomplishments, and goals. Whether you are posting about your school projects, volunteering experiences, or hobbies, each post adds to the picture of who you are. Creating a strong online presence can help you catch the eye of future employers when they look at your personal and professional social media profiles. For example, imagine yourself as an architect crafting a masterpiece — a digital identity that reflects your personality, passions, and professional aspirations. Sculpture your online persona with meticulous care and intentionality. Cultivating a compelling online presence is akin to sculpting your brand. Whether optimizing your social media profile, curating engaging content for social media platforms, or launching your professional website, each element contributes to your digital persona and identity.

Keep in mind that your digital footprint extends far beyond graduation day. Just as a well-designed building stands the test of time, your online presence can shape your professional trajectory for years. Continuously refine and update your digital identity as you grow and evolve in your career. Embrace feedback and seek opportunities to learn and adapt to the ever-changing digital media landscape. By nurturing your digital persona, you will lay the foundation for a successful and fulfilling future in the digital age.

Managing Your Digital Footprint.

Imagine your digital footprint as a trail of breadcrumbs scattered across the vast expanse of the internet—a testament to your online presence and activities. Every click, comment, and post leaves a lasting impression, shaping perceptions and influencing outcomes. It is imperative to tread carefully and be mindful of the ramifications of your digital actions. Adopt a proactive approach to managing your digital footprint by safeguarding your reputation, protecting your privacy, and navigating the digital landscape with confidence and integrity.

Furthermore, consider your digital footprint as an extension of your brand. Just as a company carefully cultivates its brand image to appeal to its target audience, curate your online presence to reflect the values and qualities you wish to convey. Consistency is key — ensure that your digital persona aligns with your offline identity and aspirations. Whether you're showcasing your professional accomplishments on a particular social media platform, maintain a cohesive narrative that reinforces your brand and distinguishes you from the digital noise.

Recognize the permanence of your digital footprint in an era where information is archived and readily accessible. Even seemingly innocuous posts or comments from years past can resurface and impact your reputation in unforeseen ways. Consider caution before sharing sensitive information or engaging in controversial discussions online. Remember that what you post today could have far-reaching consequences tomorrow. By exercising discretion and foresight in your digital interactions, you'll minimize the risk of encountering future pitfalls or regrets.

Networking and Relationship Building.

Close your eyes and envision a vast digital landscape teeming with opportunities for connection and collaboration. Social media platforms serve as virtual playgrounds where serendipitous encounters and meaningful interactions abound. By embracing the art of digital networking, you can forge lasting relationships, glean invaluable insights, and expand your professional horizons. From engaging with industry thought leaders to participating in online communities, professional opportunities are boundless (Castillo De Mesa et al., 2019). Let's navigate this digital ecosystem together, harnessing its potential to cultivate meaningful connections and propel your career forward.

Envision social media as a big, virtual party where you can meet people with similar interests and goals. By connecting with people online, you can build a network of friends, mentors, and professionals who can serve as resources throughout your life's journey. Like making friends in person, building relationships online takes time and effort. Start by reaching out to people who inspire you or share your passions. Engage with their posts, share your thoughts, and don't be afraid to initiate conversations. You never know where these connections might lead you—in school, your career, or life.

Fancy a vast digital landscape seething with opportunities for connection and collaboration. Social media has become integral to our daily lives, influencing personal interactions and professional dynamics. In today's fast-paced world, social media platforms are powerful tools for networking, personal branding, and job searching.

Maintaining a professional online presence is crucial for recent graduates, as employers often review social media profiles as part of the hiring process. Best practices include regularly updating social media profiles with relevant experiences, sharing industry-specific content to demonstrate expertise, and engaging with professional networks. According to a 2017 study by iCIMS, a leading cloud-based talent acquisition solutions provider, 70% of employers use social networking sites to research candidates during hiring (iCIMS, 2017).

Embrace the spirit of community and collaboration on social media platforms to expand your network and enrich your professional experience. Engage in conversations, participate in industry-specific groups, and contribute valuable insights and perspectives to the collective discourse. By actively participating in online communities, you'll enhance your visibility and credibility and access invaluable resources, mentorship opportunities, and potential collaborators. Cultivate a spirit of generosity and reciprocity, offering support and encouragement to your peers and celebrating their successes as your own.

As you traverse the digital landscape, it is essential to approach networking with authenticity and intentionality, especially while nurturing friendships and cultivating genuine connections by engaging in meaningful conversations, whether in person or online. Networking is not just about collecting contacts. It is about taking the initiative to follow up on new contacts to build and sustain quality relationships. Take the time to listen and contribute to conversations, positioning yourself as a valuable resource and trusted ally.

While strategic networking is essential, some of the most valuable connections can arise unexpectedly. For example, your goals should be identical for in-person and digital networking. There is an art to it. With your goals in mind, strategically build a platform to promote yourself by knowing when and how to post content. The purpose of this is to attract what you are hoping to become.

Leverage the power of digital storytelling to craft a compelling narrative that resonates with your audience. Your digital footprint is not just a collection of random data points. It is a story waiting to be told. Use multimedia platforms such as blogs, vlogs, or digital portfolios to visually showcase your journey, achievements, and aspirations authentically and visually engagingly. You'll create a compelling digital identity that captivates and inspires others by weaving your experiences, passions, and goals into a cohesive narrative. Embrace the art of digital storytelling as a powerful tool for shaping perceptions, building connections, and leaving a lasting impact in the digital realm.

There are expectations when connecting with professionals online (Zhang & Benayoun, 2020). Write and publish a brief and impactful professional narrative of yourself as an introduction. Post an above-the-shoulder photograph as a visual introduction to who you are. That profile photo and the banner image behind you are everything. To prepare for your photo, take the time to groom yourself and wear any color except for red. You don't want to come off as aggressive or distracting. Wear neutral colors- blue, gray, or white. Consider wearing a tie or a bow tie, depending on your style. Minimize any jewelry or makeup and allow your heart to speak.

The online content you present will help immerse other professionals in who you are and where you want to be. Recognizing and researching these tips will add value to your professional identity. The earlier you know and do this often, the better. You have a brand to protect. You are a brand. You have a brain with a degree that you must market to impact lives. Do your homework and learn more about these tips beyond this book by searching for more digital resources on networking.

Be open to new opportunities and experiences and proactive in seeking diverse perspectives. Priorities are key. Consider which is most important: purchasing your favorite pair of shoes or a student-discounted membership to a professional community. You decide what you want career-wise. It is your choice. Nurture your skill sets. Participate in virtual events, forums, and interest groups. Be curious and adventurous in your digital endeavors. You never know where a chance encounter or a shared interest may lead, so embrace the unpredictability of the digital playground with enthusiasm and optimism.

Digital networking is a two-way street. As you seek support and guidance, generously offer your assistance and expertise to those in your network. Please pay it forward by championing and mentoring aspiring professionals while sharing valuable resources. A spirit of generosity and reciprocity in your digital interactions will strengthen your connections and contribute to your professional community's collective growth and success. Together, let's harness the power of digital networking to create a vibrant ecosystem of collaboration, innovation, and mutual support.

Leveraging Technology for Learning and Growth.

Knowledge is no longer confined to the boundaries of traditional brick and mortars. It is accessible at your fingertips, waiting to be discovered and embraced. Through the marvels of technology, you can embark on a lifelong learning journey, enriching your mind and honing your skills with unprecedented ease. From immersive online courses to interactive educational apps, the digital landscape is ripe with opportunities for growth and self-improvement.

As you step into the vast realm of digital learning, it is crucial to approach it with curiosity and discernment. With many online resources, it is easy to become overwhelmed by the sheer volume of information. Take the time to discern credible sources from unreliable ones. Prioritize quality over quantity in your quest for knowledge (Prike, Butler, & Ecker, 2024). Find reputable platforms and educators who can provide valuable insights and guidance on your learning journey. By cultivating a discerning eye and a critical mindset, you'll navigate the digital landscape with confidence and clarity (Zauner & Karp, 2020).

Moreover, embrace the spirit of lifelong learning as a cornerstone of your personal and professional development. The digital age offers unparalleled opportunities for continuous growth and adaptation, allowing you to stay ahead of the curve in an ever-changing world. Invest in your education and skill development regularly, whether it is through formal courses, self-paced tutorials, or peer-to-peer learning networks.

As previously explained, embracing a growth mindset and remaining open to new ideas and perspectives will allow you to succeed in an increasingly competitive and dynamic job market.

Finally, remember that learning extends beyond the confines of traditional educational formats. Embrace unconventional learning experiences and explore interdisciplinary subjects that spark your curiosity and ignite your passion. Whether it is delving into art, science, technology, or humanities, allow yourself the freedom to explore diverse interests and cultivate a well-rounded intellect.

The digital landscape is your playground for intellectual exploration and discovery, so seize the opportunity to broaden your horizons and expand your worldview. With dedication, perseverance, and a thirst for knowledge, the possibilities for growth and self-improvement in the digital age are limitless.

Thus, being mindful of one's digital footprint and leveraging social media strategically can significantly enhance career prospects and professional development. Social media platforms serve as conduits for forging genuine relationships, exchanging insights, and expanding professional horizons.

Harnessing Social Media for Career Advancement.

A solid social media presence in the competitive workplace can be a powerful asset, opening doors to new opportunities and propelling your career to new heights. By strategically leveraging social media platforms, you can showcase your skills, amplify your achievements, and position yourself as a thought leader. From crafting compelling social media profiles to engaging with industry influencers, the possibilities for career advancement are boundless. Let's embark on this journey together, harnessing the power of social media to chart a course toward professional success.

Moreover, stay abreast of emerging trends and best practices in social media marketing and personal branding to maintain a competitive edge in the digital landscape. Social media platforms constantly evolve, with new features, algorithms, and strategies shaping how users engage and interact online. Dedicate time to staying informed and experimenting with different tactics to optimize your social media presence for maximum impact. Whether harnessing the power of video content, mastering the art of storytelling, or leveraging data analytics to track your performance, continuously refine and adapt your approach to stay ahead of the curve.

Lastly, be mindful of social media use's potential pitfalls and risks, from privacy concerns to online harassment and misinformation. Exercise caution when sharing personal information or engaging in sensitive discussions and familiarize yourself with privacy settings and security measures to protect your digital identity.

Practice digital hygiene by regularly auditing your social media profiles, cleaning up outdated or irrelevant content, and managing your online reputation proactively. Navigating the digital landscape with vigilance and discernment will mitigate potential risks and ensure your social media presence positively influences your career advancement and personal growth.

Cultivating Digital Leadership.

In today's digitally driven world, the mantle of leadership extends beyond traditional hierarchies and organizational structures. It is about influence, impact, and inspiration—qualities that transcend boundaries and resonate across the digital landscape.

As aspiring leaders, we must embrace the ethos of digital leadership, embodying traits such as authenticity, empathy, and innovation in our online interactions. By leading by example and harnessing the power of technology for positive change, we can usher in a new era of digital leadership—one defined by integrity, resilience, and vision.

Moreover, effective digital leadership entails fostering a culture of inclusivity and diversity in online spaces. Embrace the opportunity to amplify underrepresented voices and advocate for equity and inclusion in all aspects of digital discourse. Actively seek out diverse perspectives and experiences and create inclusive environments where everyone feels valued and respected. By championing diversity and equity in your online interactions, you'll enrich the dialogue and inspire others to do the same, driving meaningful change and progress in the digital realm.

The Erik Qualman quote, *"We don't have a choice on whether we do social media, the question is how well we do it,"* encapsulates the role of social media and technology in shaping our lives and careers. It underscores the inevitability of engaging with these digital platforms and the importance of doing so with purpose and intentionality. As graduating college seniors are poised to enter the workforce or pursue higher education, we must recognize the transformative potential of social media and technology in our personal and professional lives.

Readers, I urge you to view social media and technology not just as tools for entertainment or communication but as powerful instruments for empowerment and self-expression. Seize the opportunity to leverage these platforms to amplify your voice, showcase your talents, and connect with like-minded individuals who share your passions and aspirations. Embrace the freedom and creativity of social media and technology to craft a digital presence that authentically reflects who you are and what you stand for.

However, with great power comes great responsibility. As you navigate the digital landscape, remember to use these tools responsibly and ethically. Respect the privacy and dignity of others, critically evaluate the information you encounter online, and strive to contribute positively to digital conversations and communities. By upholding integrity, empathy, and accountability as principles, you will safeguard your reputation and well-being and contribute to a more inclusive, ethical, and prosperous digital society. As you embark on this journey into the digital age, may you harness the full potential of social media and technology to achieve personal and professional success while positively impacting the world around you.

Furthermore, cultivate a growth mindset and a willingness to embrace failure as a tipping point to success as a digital leader (Foster, 2022). The fast-paced nature of the digital landscape demands adaptability and resilience in the face of adversity. Don't be afraid to take calculated risks, experiment with new ideas, and learn from setbacks. View challenges as opportunities for growth and innovation and approach them with determination and optimism.

Demonstrating resilience and perseverance in the face of obstacles will inspire others to do the same and foster a culture of continuous improvement and innovation in the digital community.

Lead with purpose and clear vision in your digital leadership endeavors. Define your values, goals, and priorities, and align your actions with your vision for positive change and impact. Whether it is advocating for social justice, driving sustainability initiatives, or promoting ethical practices in technology, articulate your mission and rally others around a shared sense of purpose. By leading with vision and conviction, you'll galvanize support, mobilize resources, and drive meaningful progress toward a brighter future in the digital age. Embrace the responsibility and opportunity of digital leadership with passion and purpose, and together, let's shape a more inclusive, innovative, and sustainable digital landscape for generations to come.

CHAPTER 6

The BIG fuss about networking

"Instead of better glasses, your network gives you better eyes" (Garner, 2017).

Ronald Stuart Burt

Dr. Burt is an American sociologist and the Hobart W. Williams Professor of Sociology and Strategy at the University of Chicago Booth School of Business. He is most notable for his research and writing on social networks and social capital, particularly the concept of structural holes in a social network.

As I reflect on my journey through the maze of professional growth, one truth stands out like a beacon guiding me through the fog: networking isn't just a buzzword. It is the compass that steers us toward our aspirations. Visualize this: a young graduate, fresh-faced and eager, stepping into the world of opportunities. That was me. Armed with degrees and ambitions, I embarked on this journey, believing that success was solely a result of individual prowess. Oh, how mistaken I was until I truly grasped the profound significance of networking.

"Instead of better glasses, your network gives you better eyes" (Garner, 2017). The words of Ronald Stuart Burt, an American sociologist and the Hobart W. Williams Professor of Sociology and Strategy at the University of Chicago Booth School of Business, struck a chord in me, unraveling growth, resilience, and enlightenment. Allow me to guide you through this chapter, not as an instructor but as a fellow traveler who has traversed the winding paths of networking and learning invaluable lessons. Let us embark on a journey that will

221

transform your perception of networking, empowering you to harness its boundless potential.

Networking: Beyond Business Cards.

Your network is of value if you know how to be "friendly but not friends" (Lampinen, McMillan, Brown, Faraj, Cambazoglu, & Virtala, 2017, p. 170). When I first heard of networking, I imagined stiff suits, awkward handshakes, and a stack of business cards exchanged in sterile conference rooms. But oh, how wrong I was! Networking is so much more than superficial exchanges. It is about building genuine connections that can shape your future. You see, networking is like planting seeds in a garden. At first, they may seem small and insignificant, but with care and nurturing, they grow into flourishing relationships, bearing fruits of opportunity. Through networking, I discovered that every interaction, no matter how fleeting, holds the potential to spark something meaningful.

As I delved deeper into building my network, I quickly realized it was not enough to collect contacts simply. I needed to nurture genuine relationships. I learned the importance of investing time and effort into cultivating connections and transforming weak ties into strong bonds. It wasn't just about exchanging pleasantries at networking events or sending generic social media requests. It was about making meaningful connections based on shared interests, values, and goals. I discovered that authenticity is the key to forging lasting relationships. People are more likely to engage and support you when they sense sincerity and genuine interest. By investing in profound, meaningful connections, I was surrounded by a supportive community of allies who championed my growth and success.

Networking: From Acquaintances to Allies.

Delving deeper into the world of networking, I realize that it is not just about collecting contacts. It is about cultivating a community of allies who have your back.

Networking is a journey, not a destination. It is about building relationships that evolve and strengthen over time. I vividly remember attending my first networking event, feeling like a fish out of water in a sea of unfamiliar faces. But with each conversation, I gained confidence and insight. I discovered networking as a two-way street. It is not about what you gain but what you offer (Ibarra & Hunter, 2007). By embracing the ethos of reciprocity, I forged connections that transcended transactional exchanges, paving the way for meaningful collaborations and mutual support.

Through my own experiences, I understand the profound truth behind these words. Your network isn't just a collection of names in your contacts list. It is a lens through which you view the world. Similar to a prism, it refracts perspectives, illuminating opportunities once obscured. Thus, our network isn't just a passive entity. It shapes our perceptions, influences our decisions, and broadens our horizons.

Through interactions with others, we gain new insights, challenge our assumptions, and discover paths we never knew existed. By embracing the diversity and richness of our networks, we open ourselves up to a world of endless possibilities, where every connection is a potential catalyst for growth and discovery.

Mapping Your Social Network.

I identified and understood who was already in my circle when I began my networking journey. Like exploring a new territory, I mapped out my social landscape, identifying friends, family, classmates, colleagues, and acquaintances who could potentially become valuable connections. I discovered that my network wasn't limited to those I interacted with regularly. It extended to friends of friends, alum networks, and even online communities. By recognizing the breadth and depth of my network, I could pinpoint areas where I could expand and diversify my connections, laying the groundwork for future growth and opportunities.

Cultivating Meaningful Relationships.

During my networking journey, I have learned a valuable lesson. It is not about the sheer number of connections you have collected but the depth and quality of those relationships. I used to believe that the more contacts I amassed, the better my chances of success. However, I soon realized that having a hundred superficial connections pales to having a handful of deep, meaningful relationships. Quality trumps quantity every time. Instead of spreading myself thin and maintaining countless acquaintances, I focused on nurturing a few select relationships built on mutual trust, respect, and support.

Meaningful relationships are like seeds. They require care, attention, and time to flourish. While invested in building rapport, actively listening, and offering support to those within my network, I found that these connections were personally fulfilling and professionally beneficial. The people in my network would go the extra mile to help me, offer valuable

226

insights, and open doors to opportunities I wouldn't have found on my own. By prioritizing quality over quantity, I cultivated a network that was not only robust but also genuinely enriching, both professionally and personally.

Structural Holes: Opportunities in Gaps.

Understanding the concept of structural holes was like unlocking a hidden treasure chest in networking. I learned that structural holes represent gaps or spaces between individuals or groups in a network. Initially, I saw these gaps as obstacles, areas where connections were lacking. However, I soon realized that these structural holes were not barriers but opportunities waiting to be seized. By bridging these gaps, I positioned myself as a valuable intermediary, connecting disparate groups and facilitating the flow of information and resources. Instead of fearing these structural holes, I learned to embrace them as gateways to new opportunities and collaborations.

Furthermore, understanding the concept of structural holes reshaped my approach to networking. Instead of strengthening existing connections, I intentionally sought out these gaps. I identified areas where there was a lack of communication or collaboration between different areas of my network. Then, I strategically positioned myself to bridge these structural holes, acting as a conduit for information and opportunities. By doing so, I expanded my network and became a valuable resource for others, earning their trust and respect in the process.

Embracing the concept of structural holes allowed me to see networking as more than just a series of transactions; it became a journey of exploration and discovery. I learned to seek opportunities where others saw obstacles, leveraging my unique position to create value for myself and those around me. I gained insights, forged connections, and unlocked new possibilities with each structural hole I bridged. It was a journey filled with challenges and triumphs, but through it all, I developed a deeper understanding of the transformative power of networking.

Harnessing Diversity: The Power of Perspectives.

As a foreign-American, I've come to appreciate the immense value of diversity in shaping our perspectives and driving innovation. Diversity goes beyond surface-level differences. It encompasses a rich tapestry of experiences, backgrounds, and perspectives. Whether it is engaging with individuals from different cultural backgrounds, generations, or industries, I've found that embracing diversity enriches every interaction and fuels creativity and problem-solving. In the workplace, diversity isn't just a buzzword. It is a catalyst for progress and transformation. By bringing together individuals with diverse experiences and perspectives, organizations can tap into a wealth of insights and ideas that drive innovation and success.

As an immigrant, I understand firsthand the challenges and opportunities of navigating diverse environments.

I've learned to leverage my unique perspective as a bridge between different cultures and communities, fostering understanding and collaboration. By embracing my cultural heritage and sharing my experiences with others, I have built authentic connections and contributed to creating inclusive and equitable workplaces. I've seen how diversity fosters a sense of belonging and empowers individuals to bring their whole selves to work, driving creativity, productivity, and organizational success.

However, harnessing the power of diversity isn't without its challenges. It requires a commitment to equity, inclusion, and justice, ensuring that every voice is heard and valued. It means creating environments where individuals feel safe to express themselves and where differences are celebrated rather than stifled. By championing diversity and fostering a culture of belonging, organizations can unleash the full potential of their workforce, driving innovation and creating lasting impact. As I continue networking, I remain committed to promoting diversity, equity, and inclusion in every interaction, knowing that it is the right thing to do and essential for driving positive change in the world.

Effective Communication: The Art of Connection.

Mastering the art of effective communication has been a game-changer in my networking journey. It is not just about speaking; it is about genuinely connecting with others on a deeper level. I've learned that effective communication isn't just about what you say and how you listen. By practicing active listening and empathy, I've forged genuine connections with people from all walks of life. I've discovered that communication isn't just a tool for conveying information; it is a bridge that connects hearts and minds. Through open, honest, and meaningful conversations, I've built trust, fostered understanding, and laid the foundation for lasting relationships.

Networking Events: Maximizing Every Opportunity.

Networking events can be intimidating but are invaluable opportunities to expand your network and explore new possibilities. I've learned to approach these events strategically, setting clear goals and objectives beforehand. Whether it is attending industry conferences, meetups, or social gatherings, I've found that preparation is key. I've made the most of every opportunity by researching attendees, topics, and potential conversation starters. Networking events are not just about collecting business cards or making small talk; they build meaningful connections and foster genuine relationships. By being genuine, approachable, and curious, I've been able to turn networking events into springboards for growth and opportunities.

Digital Networking: Leveraging Social Media.

In today's digital age, leveraging social media and online platforms has become indispensable in networking. I've found that these virtual spaces offer boundless opportunities to connect with professionals, share insights, and showcase your expertise. There's a plethora of platforms waiting to be explored. I've learned to harness the power of digital networking by curating a professional online presence that reflects my skills, interests, and aspirations. By sharing valuable content, engaging with thought leaders, and participating in relevant conversations, I've expanded my network beyond geographical boundaries and tapped into a global community of like-minded individuals.

However, navigating the digital landscape comes with its own set of challenges. With the sheer volume of information and interactions online, it is easy to get lost in the noise. That's why I've learned to be intentional and strategic in my digital networking efforts. I've focused on building authentic connections rather than amassing followers or connections. I've also been mindful of maintaining a balance between online and offline interactions, recognizing that authentic relationships are forged through meaningful conversations and genuine connections. By leveraging social media and online platforms thoughtfully and strategically, I've amplified my networking efforts and unlocked new opportunities in ways I never thought possible.

Network Maintenance: Keeping Relationships Alive.

Maintaining relationships in your network is just as crucial as building them in the first place. I've learned that consistent effort and communication are vital to keeping connections alive. Whether sending a quick check-in email, meeting for coffee, or simply engaging with someone's posts on social media, I've prioritized staying connected with my network. I've found that small gestures of appreciation and support go a long way in nurturing relationships and keeping them strong over time. By staying proactive and attentive to the needs and interests of those in my network, I've fostered trust and loyalty, ensuring that my connections remain valuable allies throughout my career journey.

Paying It Forward: The Reciprocity of Networking.

One of the most rewarding aspects of networking is the opportunity to pay it forward and help others. Networking isn't just about what you can gain. It is also about what you can give back to the community. Whether offering mentorship to a junior colleague, making introductions, or sharing insights and resources, I've found fulfillment in supporting others and contributing to their success. I've seen firsthand how acts of generosity and kindness create a ripple effect, strengthening the fabric of our professional community. By embracing the ethos of reciprocity, I've cultivated a culture of collaboration and mutual support within my network, where we all thrive together.

Scaling Up: Growing Your Network Over Time.

Building a network isn't just a one-time task. It is an ongoing process that requires dedication and perseverance. I've learned that my network should also develop and reflect my evolving goals and aspirations as I grow in my profession. Building a network is like tending to a garden - as the seasons change, new opportunities bloom, but it is up to the gardener to cultivate and nurture those seeds.

By actively seeking out new relationships, staying engaged with existing contacts, and remaining open to new experiences, I've scaled up my network and unlocked doors to exciting opportunities I never thought possible. Each new connection brings fresh perspectives, valuable insights, and potential collaborations, enriching my personal and professional life. Through continuous growth and expansion, I've built a network that serves as a foundation for my success and a source of support and inspiration throughout my journey.

Networking for Introverts.

As an introvert during my undergraduate years in Pennsylvania, I initially found networking daunting. I still consider myself an introvert in some ways. The thought of striking up conversations with strangers and navigating significant networking events filled me with anxiety. However, I quickly realized that networking isn't about being the loudest voice in the room. It is about making genuine and authentic connections. Leveraging my strengths as an introvert helped me focus on one-on-one conversations and build deeper connections with individuals over time. By setting small, achievable goals and gradually pushing myself out of my comfort zone, I discovered that networking could be an enriching experience, even for the reserved people among us. It is okay to be an introvert. However, you must also know when to exercise extrovert qualities (code-switching, adapting to your environment, growing your professional identity). Both are beneficial.

Turning Setbacks into Opportunities.

I've encountered my fair share of rejection and setbacks in my networking journey. Whether it is a cold response to an email or a missed opportunity, rejection can sting and shake your confidence. However, I've learned to reframe rejection as a learning opportunity and a facilitation to growth. Instead of dwelling on disappointment, I use rejection as fuel to propel me forward. I analyze what went wrong, identify areas for improvement, and adapt my approach accordingly. Resilience is key in navigating the ups and downs of networking. By embracing rejection as a natural part of the process and maintaining a positive mindset, I've been able to bounce back stronger and more determined than ever before.

In addition to the strategies discussed in this chapter, I encourage recent graduates to explore resources like my podcast, *The Ability Project*, available on most podcast media platforms. In this podcast, I've had the privilege of interviewing hiring professionals and leaders from around the world, gaining valuable insights and advice on navigating the challenges of the job market. Listening to these conversations can provide invaluable guidance and inspiration, helping you to approach rejection as a learning opportunity and turn setbacks into opportunities for growth. So, I invite you to tune in to *The Ability Project* and join me on a journey of discovery and empowerment as we navigate the world of networking and professional development together.

Avoiding Networking Burnout.

Networking burnout is a real challenge that many professionals face, myself included. At times, networking can seem like a never-ending cycle of events, meetings, and follow-ups, leading to feeling drained and overwhelmed. However, I have learned to be selective and intentional about where I invest my time and energy instead of trying to attend every event or accept every connection request. By prioritizing quality interactions over sheer quantity, I maintain a sense of purpose and fulfillment in my networking efforts.

One strategy to help avoid networking burnout is setting boundaries and establishing clear goals for my networking activities. By defining what success looks like for me, whether making a certain number of meaningful connections or pursuing specific opportunities, I can focus my efforts on activities that align with my objectives. I have also learned to listen to my body and mind, recognizing when to take a step back and recharge. Taking breaks, practicing self-care, and cultivating hobbies outside of work have been instrumental in preventing burnout and maintaining a healthy work-life balance.

Moreover, delegation and collaboration are equally important in managing networking responsibilities. Instead of trying to complete tasks independently, I've learned to leverage the support of colleagues, mentors, and peers. Whether dividing networking tasks among team members or seeking guidance from experienced professionals, collaboration has allowed me to share the workload and gain valuable insights and support. By working smarter, not harder, I avoid the burnout that sustains my networking efforts over the long term.

Reflecting on my networking journey, I'm reminded of the profound wisdom in Ronald Stuart Burt's quote, "Instead of better glasses, your network gives you better eyes." This quote encapsulates the essence of networking. It is not just about what you know but who you know and how you leverage those connections to gain new perspectives and opportunities.

Throughout this chapter, I've shared my experiences and lessons learned in building and nurturing my network, from understanding the importance of quality over quantity to embracing diversity and overcoming challenges like networking burnout. Each interaction, whether in person or online, has expanded my horizons and enriched my professional journey.

Navigating networking complexities clarifies one truth: our network is our greatest asset, offering support, inspiration, and opportunities, empowering us to achieve dreams; by embracing its power, we unlock new possibilities, regardless of personality or experience, shaping our future with confidence and gaining better perspective with each connection.

CHAPTER 7

Dealing with those student loans ...

"You may have to fight a battle more than once to win it" (Hennessey, 2014).

Margaret Thatcher

Margaret Thatcher was a British stateswoman who served as Prime Minister of the United Kingdom from 1979 to 1990.

As I stood on the brink of completing the final year of my doctorate, a sense of accomplishment mingled with a cloud of uncertainty. The weight of an impending battle against student loans overshadowed the anticipation of embarking on a new chapter of life. Margaret Thatcher, a wise stateswoman who once led the United Kingdom, noted that achieving victory might require repeated efforts (Hennessey, 2014). These words echoed in my mind as I delved into the world of student loan relief, determined to conquer this financial obstacle that threatened to hinder my dreams. Drawing inspiration from Thatcher's quote, we will navigate this landscape together, armed with knowledge, resilience, and the belief that victory is possible.

In this chapter, I'll talk about the tough journey of dealing with student loans and ways to ease that burden. Before diving in, it's important to look for opportunities that match your skills—like scholarships. Scholarships can help pay for college and reduce the amount you need to borrow. Below, I'll share my tips on how to find and manage scholarships, as well as how to handle student loans effectively.

Find Scholarships That Fit!

College can be a huge financial burden, and it's important to start searching for scholarships as soon as possible. Many students wait until their senior year, but the earlier you begin, the more options you'll find. Scholarships can come from various places, including local organizations, schools, and even online databases. By applying to multiple scholarships, you increase your chances of receiving financial aid, which can significantly reduce your overall college costs. Education is expensive; look for scholarships early and often.

In addition to traditional scholarships, look for unique opportunities that cater to your interests or background. For example, some scholarships are available for students pursuing specific majors or those who have overcome certain challenges. Keep an organized list of deadlines and requirements, and don't hesitate to ask teachers or mentors for help in finding scholarships that fit you. The effort you put in now can pay off tremendously later.

Save Big with Community Colleges.

Starting your education at a community college can be a smart financial move. Community colleges typically offer lower tuition rates, allowing you to complete your general education requirements without breaking the bank. This can give you a solid foundation before transferring to a four-year university for your major. By taking advantage of the lower costs at community college, you can save a significant amount of money while still earning credits that will count toward your degree.

Moreover, community colleges often have smaller class sizes, which can lead to more personalized attention from instructors. This supportive environment can help you adjust to college-level coursework and give you the confidence to succeed in your future studies. Once you've completed your pre-requisites, you can transfer to your desired university, bringing with you both valuable credits and a lighter financial burden.

Affordable Pathways.

When planning your education, consider starting at a college with lower tuition that offers programs similar to your desired major. Many state universities and smaller colleges provide quality education at a fraction of the cost of larger institutions. By enrolling in one of these schools, you can earn your degree without accumulating excessive debt. Once you've proven yourself academically, you can transfer to a more prestigious university to complete your education.

Transferring can also give you the advantage of having a more diverse college experience. You'll gain new perspectives and make connections at different institutions, which can enrich your education.

Remember to research transfer agreements between schools, as many colleges have partnerships that facilitate a smoother transition and ensure that your credits will be accepted.

Careers That Pay Back.

An option to explore is programs designed to help reduce student debt, especially in specific professional fields. For instance, medical doctors who choose to serve in rural or underserved areas can qualify for loan forgiveness programs that erase a portion of their student loans after a certain number of years of practice. This not only helps alleviate the financial burden but also addresses critical healthcare needs in communities that often lack access to medical services.

Additionally, don't overlook employer repayment assistance programs. Some employers offer student loan repayment assistance as part of their benefits package, which can significantly help reduce your debt

(Half, 2024). State-specific programs and scholarships are also worth exploring. Many states provide loan repayment assistance for residents in particular professions, such as healthcare or education. Various organizations offer scholarships and grants specifically for loan repayment, often based on your career path or qualifications (NFCC, n.d.).

Similarly, teachers who commit to working in low-income schools may also benefit from loan forgiveness programs. By dedicating a few years to teaching in these areas, they can have a significant portion of their student debt forgiven (Looney, 2022; Wu, 2020). Other professions, such as social workers and public health officials, often have access to similar relief programs, promoting careers that support the community while helping graduates manage their finances. These programs can significantly lighten your financial load after graduation, allowing you to focus on your career rather than being overwhelmed by debt. Research the eligibility requirements for these programs early on, and consider how your career choices can align with opportunities for debt relief.

Financial Wisdom: Your Guide to Smart Choices.

It's wise to consult with a financial advisor during your college years. Many banks and credit unions offer free financial counseling for students. A financial advisor can help you understand your options for managing tuition costs, budgeting, and planning for the future. They can also guide you through the ins and outs of student loans, helping you make informed decisions about borrowing.

These professionals have the expertise and experience to provide valuable insights and advice tailored to your situation. They can assist with steering the intricacies of loan repayment options, understand the long-term implications of your decisions, and develop a personalized strategy for managing your student debt.

Additionally, a financial advisor can assist you in creating a plan for after graduation, including how to manage your loan repayments. By having a clear financial strategy, you can avoid falling into debt traps and ensure that you're on the right path toward financial stability.

Lastly, financial counseling and educational resources should be made use of. Non-profit credit counseling agencies, such as the National Foundation for Credit Counseling (NFCC), offer free or low-cost services to help you manage your debt. The Consumer Financial Protection Bureau (CFPB) also provides resources and tools for dealing with student loans (CFPB, n.d.). By exploring these resources, college students and recent graduates can uncover numerous options to help manage and repay their loans, paving the way for a more secure financial future.

Advice for Loans.

Now that we've covered scholarships and ways to reduce your education costs, it's essential to address the topic of student loans. While loans can sometimes feel like a necessary evil in funding your education, understanding how to manage them wisely can make a significant difference in your post-college life. In the following sections, I'll provide practical advice on how to navigate student loans, including strategies for borrowing wisely and tips for repayment.

Understanding the Student Loan Landscape.

As a college student in a world of student loans, we cannot ignore the rising concern surrounding this financial burden. The student loan crisis, a staggering reality, continues to burden students as they struggle to find their footing in the post-graduation world (Nica & Mirică, 2017). As a student, the stories of countless individuals grappling with loan repayments painted a picture of financial hardship and limited opportunities. It has become clear that understanding the intricacies of this crisis was crucial in charting a path toward relief and success.

In my quest for knowledge, I discovered the two main types of student loans: federal and private. Federal loans, backed by the government, offered advantages such as lower interest rates and flexible repayment options. On the other hand, private loans, provided by banks and other financial institutions, came with their own set of terms and conditions. Navigating the intricacies of these loan types became essential in determining the most suitable path toward managing my student debt.

Armed with a desire to understand the true impact of student loan debt, I delved into the statistics surrounding this issue. Nationally, the numbers were staggering, revealing the heavy burden shouldered by graduates (Kantrowitz, 2012). The weight of debt can influence career choices, delay significant life milestones, and even impact mental and emotional well-being. It became clear that the battle for relief was not just about financial freedom but also about reclaiming control over our lives and pursuing our dreams without the constant worry of debt.

Federal loans, such as Stafford or Perkins loans, offered various benefits, including fixed interest rates and potential eligibility for loan forgiveness programs. Subsidized loans provided relief during the grace period and while enrolled in school. On the other hand, private loans, though lacking some of the advantages of federal loans, offered alternative solutions tailored to individual financial circumstances. Understanding the nuances of subsidized and unsubsidized loans and the potential benefits of federal and private loan options are crucial in crafting a strategic approach to managing my student loan debt.

As I learned more about student loans, I realized the importance of familiarizing myself with loan terms, interest rates, and repayment options. Terms like a grace period, deferment, forbearance, and loan consolidation suddenly held significant weight in my journey toward relief. Interest rates played a major role in debt accumulation, making it essential to comprehend its impact on the overall repayment process. In other words, interest rates have a big impact on how much debt people collect, so it is important to understand how they affect the repayment process because even small changes can make a big difference in how much money you have to pay back. Additionally, exploring various repayment options, such as income-driven plans or extended repayment terms, allowed me to tailor my approach to suit my financial circumstances and long-term goals.

The Importance of Student Loan Relief.

In pursuit of student loan relief, find solace and inspiration in the words of Margaret Thatcher, "You may have to fight a battle more than once to win it." These powerful words resonated deeply, reminding me that the journey toward financial freedom would not be without its challenges. Thatcher's quote became my guiding light, urging me to persevere and remain resilient. It taught me that setbacks were not permanent defeats but opportunities for growth and eventual victory.

The world of student loans place an emotional and financial toll on individuals. The weight of debt creates constant anxiety and stress, casting a shadow over the joy and excitement of post-graduation life. Dreams and aspirations often took a backseat to the relentless pursuit of making loan payments.

The emotional burden is as heavy as the financial one, affecting mental well-being and hindering personal growth.

In the maze of student loans, I understand the pressing need for relief among graduates. The weight of debt stifled creativity, hindered career choices, and limited personal and professional growth opportunities.

It became clear to me in my post-doctoral years that empowering graduates with the tools and resources to tackle their student loan burdens was essential. Through education and advocacy, we must equip ourselves with the knowledge to make informed decisions and navigate the complexities of loan repayment. Specifically, by advocating for policy reform and supporting initiatives for loan forgiveness and affordable education, we could create a pathway for future generations to pursue their dreams without the shackles of overwhelming debt.

Reflecting on the significance of student loan relief, I realized it was about easing financial burdens and empowering individuals to take control of their lives. While the battle for relief is arduous, it is worth fighting for our dreams, well-being, and future.

Exploring Available Student Loan Relief Options.

In the quest for student loan relief, find federal loan programs that offer potential solutions. These programs provide various benefits to borrowers, including flexible repayment options, potential loan forgiveness, and the ability to temporarily suspend payments during financial hardship. From Direct Subsidized Loans to Parent PLUS Loans, each program has unique features and eligibility requirements.

Navigating the landscape of federal loan programs is essential in determining the most suitable path toward managing student debt.

One of the most promising options is income-driven repayment plans. These plans allow borrowers to adjust their monthly loan payments based on income and family size. It is a game-changer for those burdened with high debt levels and limited financial resources. By implementing income-driven repayment, I could ensure that my monthly payments remain manageable, allowing me to pursue my career and other financial goals. Understanding the intricacies of these plans, such as calculated payment amounts and the potential for loan forgiveness after a certain period, empowered me to make an informed decision aligned with my financial circumstances.

Managing multiple student loans and keeping track of different repayment terms and interest rates seem daunting. That's when I stumbled upon the concept of loan consolidation. Websites like NerdWallet and

Student Loan Hero offer tools and advice to help you decide if refinancing is right for you (NerdWallet, n.d.; Student Loan Hero, n.d.). Consolidating my loans allowed me to combine multiple loans into a single loan, simplifying the repayment process and potentially securing a lower interest rate. It was a practical solution that eased the administrative burden and gave me a clearer picture of my debt and repayment timeline. Understanding the pros and cons of loan consolidation gave me the confidence to explore this option and determine whether it fits my circumstances.

As I delved deeper into the available student loan relief options, I realized the importance of weighing the pros and cons of each approach. Understanding the eligibility criteria and application processes for various programs was crucial to ensure I met the requirements to benefit from these options.

I also discovered the possibility of employer-sponsored repayment assistance programs, where my employer might contribute towards my student loan payments as part of their benefits package. Furthermore, I was motivated to research scholarships, grants, and other financial aid opportunities specifically aimed at helping individuals repay their student loans. Armed with this knowledge, I was ready to navigate the vast landscape of student loan relief and find the best course of action for my journey toward financial freedom.

Proactive Strategies for Managing Student Loans.

As I confronted the reality of my student loans, I quickly realized the importance of budgeting. Creating a comprehensive financial plan became essential in managing my debt effectively. By carefully examining my income, expenses, and debt obligations, I could strategically allocate funds toward loan payments while meeting my other financial needs. Budgeting empowered me to take control of my financial situation and make conscious decisions about my spending habits. It allowed me to prioritize debt repayment and set achievable goals, bringing me one step closer to conquering my student loan burden.

In the journey to become debt-free, borrowers can discover the power of making extra payments toward their student loans. By allocating additional funds whenever possible, they can accelerate the repayment process and reduce the overall interest accrued. Every extra dollar contributed brings individuals closer to financial freedom. While it requires discipline and sacrifice, the sense of progress and the knowledge that one is actively working toward this goal can renew motivation. Through extra payments, borrowers can learn the value of persistence and the significant impact of small actions taken over time.

Exploring the option of refinancing my student loans was a significant decision that required careful consideration—refinancing involved taking out a new loan with different terms to pay off the existing ones. It could secure a lower interest rate or extend the repayment period, reducing the monthly payment amount. However, it was essential to weigh the pros and cons of refinancing, considering factors such as the impact on loan forgiveness programs, the potential loss of federal loan benefits, and the overall cost-effectiveness of the new loan terms. Through thorough research and consultation with financial advisors, I made an informed decision aligned with my long-term financial goals.

Engaging in effective communication with loan servicers was a crucial skill I learned along my journey. I contacted my loan servicers to explore potential solutions whenever I encountered financial difficulties or payment challenges. By expressing my situation honestly and articulating my needs clearly, I was often able to negotiate favorable repayment terms or secure temporary relief through options like loan deferment or forbearance. It taught me the importance of proactive communication and advocating for myself to find the best possible outcome.

Uncovering Resources to Repay College Loans.

Paying back college loans can seem overwhelming, but many resources are available to help college students and recent graduates manage their debt effectively. Knowing where to find these resources and how to use them can make a huge difference.

First, it is essential to understand the various federal loan repayment plans. The Federal Student Aid website, where the Free Application for Federal Student Aid (FAFSA) form is available, offers comprehensive information on different plans, such as the Standard Repayment Plan, which has fixed payments over ten years, and the Graduated Repayment Plan, where payments start low and increase every two years. For those looking for more flexible options, Income-Driven Repayment Plans (IDR) can cap monthly payments based on income and extend the repayment period, making payments more manageable (FSA, n.d.).

If you face temporary financial hardships, deferment and forbearance can provide relief by postponing or reducing your payments. However, it is crucial to understand that interest might still accrue during this period, which could increase your overall debt.

Advocacy and Legislative Efforts.

In the effort to overcome the burden of student loans, many individuals discover the power of collective action and advocacy. By joining forces with others who share similar experiences and frustrations, they can form a united front to push for change. Together, they amplify their voices and advocate for student loan reform. Through grassroots movements, online communities, and student organizations, graduates can work to raise awareness about the challenges faced by borrowers and the need for broader relief measures. Through collective efforts, they can begin to see the seeds of change being planted.

To make a lasting impact, it was crucial to understand the political landscape and how policy decisions were made. I delved into the intricacies of legislative processes and educated myself about policymakers who had the authority to influence student loan relief measures. By staying informed about proposed bills and policy developments, I could actively engage in discussions and shape the conversations surrounding student debt. Whether reaching out to elected representatives, attending town hall meetings, or participating in public forums, I learned that our voices could make a difference in shaping policies that directly affect our lives.

In the ever-evolving landscape of student loan relief, it is crucial to stay informed about legislative changes and policy developments. New laws and regulations could significantly impact repayment options, loan forgiveness programs, and overall borrower protections. Staying updated allowed me to adapt my strategies and take advantage of new opportunities. I made it a habit to regularly check reliable sources for news and updates related to student loans, ensuring that I was aware of any changes that could affect my repayment journey.

Advocacy for student loan reform requires strategic thinking and effective communication. Articulating our concerns and proposing practical solutions when engaging with policymakers and other influential figures were just as integral. By sharing personal stories and highlighting the broader societal impact of student loan debt, we could garner support and create a sense of urgency for change.

Overcoming Setbacks and Building Resilience.

During my journey to repay student loans, I faced numerous challenges with loan servicers. Administrative errors and technological communication breakdowns tested my patience and resolve. Despite still being in the repayment process, I found the Teacher Loan Forgiveness Program to be a good fit for my situation as an educator. Through this experience, I learned the importance of persistence and assertiveness. I meticulously documented all interactions, verified the accuracy of the provided information, and followed up on any discrepancies.

The weight of student loan debt can significantly impact mental well-being. Engaging in self-care practices and prioritizing mental health while managing debt can be beneficial. Regular exercise, mindfulness activities, and seeking support from loved ones can help maintain a positive mindset and build resilience. Additionally, accessing resources and support groups specifically geared toward those dealing with student loan debt can be invaluable. Sharing experiences and connecting with others who understand these challenges can alleviate feelings of isolation and foster a sense of solidarity. By prioritizing mental well-being, individuals can navigate the ups and downs of their repayment journey with greater strength and resilience.

Life is full of uncertainties, and unexpected circumstances can sometimes throw a wrench into our carefully crafted plans. Economic hardships, job loss, or other unforeseen events can disrupt our ability to meet our financial obligations, including student loan payments. As a result, it was crucial to remain adaptable and adjust my strategies. Reaching out to my loan servicers, I explored options such as deferment or forbearance, which provided temporary relief until I regained my financial stability.

Embracing Financial Discipline.

Accelerating my debt repayment plan, I adopted strategies to minimize discretionary expenses and maximize my income. I became more mindful of my purchases, distinguishing between wants and needs. I evaluated my spending patterns and identified areas where I could cut back without sacrificing my basic needs. I sought ways to reduce expenses, such as cooking at home instead of eating out, canceling unnecessary subscriptions, and shopping for deals and discounts. Additionally, I explored opportunities to increase my income, such as taking on a part-time job or freelancing in my field of expertise. By adopting these strategies, I gained greater control over my finances and had more resources available for my student loan payments.

As I embraced financial discipline, I realized the importance of establishing emergency savings and setting long-term financial goals. Life is filled with unexpected events, and having an emergency fund provides a safety net during challenging times.

Inspiring Success Stories.

Over the years, I have connected with graduates who successfully conquered the battle of student loan debt. Their inspirational stories offered valuable strategies, tips, and lessons that helped me to keep pushing forward.

One common thread among these success stories was the importance of seeking support from friends, family, or financial advisors. A strong support system provided encouragement and guidance during challenging times, reminding us that we were not alone in our struggles. Additionally, these graduates emphasized the significance of staying motivated and resilient. They shared strategies for maintaining a positive mindset, setting small milestones to celebrate progress, and finding inspiration for long-term goals. They also offered advice on addressing common obstacles such as unemployment, underemployment, or unexpected expenses, emphasizing the importance of adaptability and perseverance. Learning from these inspiring individuals, I gained valuable insights that helped me navigate my path to success.

Looking Toward the Future.

Reflecting on my journey, I realize the importance of equipping the next generation with financial literacy skills. Understanding personal finance and the implications of student loan debt should be integral to education. When we provide young individuals with the tools and knowledge to make informed financial decisions, we empower them to avoid excessive debt and manage their finances effectively. Advocating for financial literacy programs in schools, colleges, and universities ensures that students have the necessary skills to make sound financial choices and navigate the complexities of student loans.

Policy reform initiatives to address the student loan crisis have continued to increase as policymakers recognize the burden borrowers face and the need for comprehensive relief measures. As we look toward the future, there is hope on the horizon. Advocacy efforts, grassroots movements, and the collective voices of borrowers have brought attention to the urgency of reform. It is essential to stay engaged and support initiatives that promote fairer loan terms, increased borrower protections, and expanded loan forgiveness programs. Advocating for policy change allows us to create a more supportive and equitable system for future generations.

Despite the challenges, I remain optimistic about the future. I envision a world where the burden of student loan debt is reduced significantly, allowing individuals to pursue their dreams and contribute to society without the weight of financial strain. By advocating for change, sharing our stories, and supporting initiatives for reform, we can pave the way for a brighter tomorrow. We are creating a legacy of empowerment and opportunity for future generations as we work towards a society with reduced student loan burdens,

Many lessons can be learned, and significant progress can be made in the quest for student loan relief. While it is not an easy path, individuals often emerge stronger from experience.

Graduates are encouraged to embrace this challenge, knowing they are not alone. Seeking support, staying motivated, and addressing obstacles head-on are crucial steps. It is important to recognize the value of financial discipline, the power of advocacy, and the hope for policy reform. By sharing experiences and motivating one another, communities can work toward a brighter future where the burden of student loan debt is alleviated, allowing individuals to pursue their dreams without undue financial strain.

As Margaret Thatcher wisely observed, conquering the challenge of student loans may require persistence and determination. By understanding the landscape of student loan relief options, embracing financial discipline, and advocating for change, graduating college seniors can confidently embark on their post-education journey, knowing that the battle against student loans is worth fighting.

CHAPTER 8

How to "strategically" choose your life partner

"I'm not going to sacrifice love, real love, for any *%@$n' war or any friend, or any business, because in the end you're alone at night." (John Lennon Quotes, n.d.).

John Lennon

John Lennon was an English singer, songwriter, and peace activist who co-founded the Beatles.

In the quest for a fulfilling life, one of the most crucial decisions you'll make is choosing your life partner. John Lennon's words resonate deeply, reminding us that love remains paramount amidst the chaos of life. This chapter delves into strategically selecting a life partner—a decision that can profoundly impact your happiness, professional success, and overall well-being.

Defining Real Love.

As a graduating college senior, you are about to embark on a new chapter of your life, filled with exciting possibilities and essential decisions. Perhaps one of your most significant choices is selecting a life partner. In this chapter, I will share the wisdom I've gained over the years about strategically choosing a life partner.

Let's start by understanding the concept of real love. Real love goes beyond surface-level attraction or infatuation. It is a deep, profound connection that transcends physical appearances or fleeting emotions. Real love is built on a foundation of genuine care, respect, and understanding for one another. Physical and emotional attraction contribute to intimacy and connection. Ensure a balance of physical attraction and emotional connection, which are important for a fulfilling relationship.

To differentiate between infatuation and genuine love, it is essential to look beyond the initial rush of emotions (Baer, 2003). Infatuation often arises from external factors like physical appearance or popularity, whereas genuine love is rooted in a profound emotional bond. It is a love that withstands the test of time and remains strong even when the initial excitement fades, and obstacles arise.

Emotional connection and compatibility are crucial to real love (Marchi, Csajbók, & Jonason, 2023). It is about finding someone with similar values, goals, and aspirations. It is about having conversations that go beyond the surface and truly understanding and supporting each other on an emotional level. Having a deep emotional connection and compatibility with your partner lays a solid foundation for a lasting and fulfilling relationship.

In my journey, I've learned that real love is not just about finding the *perfect person* but being the right person. It requires a willingness to self-reflect to become the best version of ourselves in a relationship for growth. While navigating the complexities of choosing a life partner, remember to seek genuine love that goes beyond the superficial and builds on emotional connection and compatibility. Look for someone who shares your values, understands you deeply, and supports your dreams and aspirations. Real love is a beautiful and transformative force that can bring immense joy and fulfillment to your life.

Defining Your Values and Priorities.

We have explored the concept of real love. Now, let's dive into another crucial aspect of choosing your life partner: defining your values and priorities. Understand that what truly matters to you lays the foundation for finding a compatible and supportive life partner. Having aligned life goals ensures you and your partner are on the same path. Discuss your long-term plans, such as career ambitions, desire for children, and lifestyle preferences.

Ah, the exciting and sometimes perplexing quest for compatibility! As you choose a life partner, look beyond surface-level attraction for compatibility. Trust me. It is worth the effort! Compatibility prevents future conflicts and fosters a unified vision for your lives together. In my experience, I've learned that shared cultural and spiritual values are vital for a lasting and fulfilling relationship. When you and your partner have similar beliefs and principles, navigating life's challenges and making decisions together becomes easier. It fosters a sense of unity and harmony, creating a strong foundation for a successful partnership. While differences can add richness and depth to a relationship, aligned values ensure long-term compatibility and happiness.

When assessing compatibility, consider shared values, goals, and lifestyle factors. Do you both prioritize honesty, trust, and kindness? Do you both have long-term ambitions and dreams? Are they aligned? It is essential to have a solid foundation of shared values that will guide your relationship through the ups and downs of life. Aligning with your partner on core values and beliefs is essential for long-term compatibility. Discuss topics like religion, family, finances, and life goals early in the relationship. Shared values help you make consistent decisions together, preventing conflicts down the road. For instance, Dr. John Gottman's book *The Seven Principles for Making Marriage Work* emphasizes the importance of shared values in building a strong marital foundation (Gottman & Silver, 1999).

When choosing a life partner, remember to define your values and priorities. Reflect on what truly matters to you and seek a partner who shares your vision for the future. Doing so increases the likelihood of building a solid and fulfilling relationship that supports your personal growth and brings you joy and fulfillment.

Building and Sustaining Emotional Intelligence.

In the journey of choosing a life partner, one of the essential skills you can develop is emotional intelligence. Emotional intelligence is understanding and managing emotions and empathizing with others. It plays a crucial role in navigating the complexities of relationships and fostering a deep connection with your partner. Cultivating self-awareness is a fundamental aspect of emotional intelligence. Emotional intelligence is vital for effective communication and conflict resolution. Look for a partner who is self-aware, empathetic, and able to manage their emotions. This skill leads to healthier and more supportive interactions. According to Gary

Chapman in *The 5 Love Languages* (2015), understanding and expressing emotions are crucial in maintaining a loving relationship.

Take the time to reflect on your emotions, triggers, and behavior patterns. Understand and share what makes you happy, what upsets you, and how you respond to different situations. Do these in a way that does not offend or upset your partner. Share these moments in your relationships that are convenient for conversations. By better understanding yourself, you can better communicate your needs and desires to your partner.

Empathy is another vital component of emotional intelligence. It involves putting yourself in your partner's shoes and truly understanding their perspective and emotions. By practicing empathy, you can develop a deeper bond with your partner and create an environment of understanding and support. Open and honest communication is vital to resolving issues and understanding each other. Choose someone who communicates openly, listens actively, and expresses their thoughts and feelings clearly. Effective communication is a cornerstone of a strong relationship, as John Gottman and Joan DeClaire highlighted in *The Relationship Cure* (Gottman & Declaire, 2001).

Effective communication is also a skill that goes hand in hand with emotional intelligence. Learn to express your thoughts, feelings, and needs openly and honestly with your partner. Be an active listener, giving your partner your full attention and seeking to understand their point of view. Respect and trust form the foundation of any strong relationship. Ensure your partner respects your opinions, listens to you, and demonstrates trustworthiness through their actions. As noted in *The Seven Principles for Making Marriage Work*, mutual respect and trust are non-negotiable pillars of a successful partnership (Gottman & Silver, 2015).

Constructive communication refers to exchanging information, ideas, and emotions to promote mutual understanding, respect, and positive outcomes. It involves transparent, honest, and respectful dialogue to resolve conflicts, build relationships, and foster collaboration. Constructive communication helps resolve disputes, prevent misunderstandings, and strengthen the emotional connection between you and your partner (Overall, Sibley, & Travaglia, 2010).

Emotional intelligence allows you to build and maintain a healthy and fulfilling relationship. Through the development of self-awareness, empathy, and effective communication skills, my life partner, Naa Kleshie, and I have navigated challenges, expressed our needs, and deepened our bond over the years. As you choose a life partner, remember to invest in building your emotional intelligence together by cultivating self-awareness, practicing empathy, and developing effective communication skills. These qualities will enhance your relationship and contribute to your personal growth and the success of your partnership.

Seeking Compatibility.

Compatibility also extends to practical matters. Take a light-hearted inventory of your communication styles. Are you a marathon texter while your potential partner prefers face-to-face conversations? Can you both navigate misunderstandings and conflicts healthily and respectfully? How you handle disagreements can make or break a relationship. Look for a partner who approaches conflict with a problem-solving attitude rather than avoidance or aggression. This fosters a cooperative and peaceful relationship (Chapman, 2015), as emphasized in *The 5 Love Languages*. Compatibility also involves enjoying each other's company and sharing common interests. Sharing hobbies, activities, or even binge-watching the same TV shows can bring you closer together and create lasting memories. Shared interests strengthen your bond and create more opportunities for quality time together. Identify common hobbies and activities you both enjoy. While differences can be exciting, shared interests provide a foundation for companionship. So, don't forget to have some fun and laughter along the way!

Seeking compatibility goes beyond initial attraction. It is about finding someone who shares your values, communicates well, aligns with your financial attitudes, and brings joy to your life through shared interests. These little quirks can make or break the harmony in a relationship, so it is essential to find someone with whom you can communicate effectively.

Of Love and Finances.

Now, let's touch on the topic of finances. Yes, money matters! (Ward et al., 2021). Financial issues are a leading cause of marital stress and divorce. Discuss your financial habits, debt, savings, and spending priorities. Ensuring you have similar attitudes towards money management is crucial for avoiding conflicts and maintaining harmony. So, don't overlook the importance of compatibility. It is like finding the perfect puzzle piece that completes the picture of your happily ever after! Assess your compatibility in terms of financial attitudes. Are you both savers, spenders, or somewhere in between? Similar financial values and goals can prevent conflicts and help you work towards shared financial stability. But hey, it is not all seriousness and numbers!

Financial discussions can often be uncomfortable, but acknowledging each partner's spending habits, financial goals, and debt can foster understanding and collaboration. Establishing a shared budget and setting financial priorities together helps couples align their values and aspirations, creating a sense of partnership in managing their financial journey. This proactive approach can prevent misunderstandings and resentment, allowing love to flourish alongside financial stability.

Moreover, couples should be aware of the emotional aspects that money can evoke. Financial stress can strain relationships, making it essential to address any underlying concerns openly. Engaging in regular check-ins about financial health and celebrating milestones— no matter how small—can strengthen bonds and promote a sense of teamwork. By approaching finances as a shared responsibility, couples can navigate the challenges together, ensuring that love and financial well-being coexist harmoniously.

Prioritizing Love in Life's Choices.

Ah, love, that mysterious force that can turn our world upside down! As you navigate through life's choices and pursue your dreams, it is crucial to remember the importance of prioritizing love. Let's dive into this topic and see how it can shape your journey. John Lennon once said, *"All you need is love."* Now, I'm not saying you should take that literally and start serenading strangers on the street, although it might make for an intriguing story! But Lennon's assertion carries a profound truth: love is fundamental to a fulfilling life. It is what gives meaning and purpose to our endeavors.

Sometimes, we may neglect the love that nurtures our souls in pursuing external achievements and success. We get caught up in the hustle and bustle of our careers, striving for that promotion or recognition, only to realize that we've neglected the relationships that truly matter. Trust me, I've been there. Balancing personal and professional commitments is a delicate dance. It is like juggling flaming torches while riding a unicycle—challenging but not impossible. The key is to recognize our love for self, and others deserve a prime spot on our priority list.

Success means little if we don't have the warmth and support of love in our lives. It is about finding that sweet spot where we pursue our passions and ambitions while nurturing our relationships and making time for those we care about. So, my dear graduates, remember to prioritize love as you embark on this exciting phase of life. It is the glue that holds everything together, the sprinkle of magic that makes the journey worthwhile. Pursue your dreams and chase your ambitions, but always make room in your heart and schedule for love. Moreover, who knows, maybe one day, you'll see yourself serenading someone on the street and living your very own love story!

Balancing Love and Professional Commitments.

Finding a balance between personal and professional commitments while nurturing love is indeed a delicate art, but fear not! I've gathered some insights from my journey and experiences to guide you in this balancing act.

First and foremost, it is crucial to set priorities and establish boundaries. Take the time to reflect on what truly matters to you and identify your non-negotiables. By understanding your values and priorities, you can make conscious decisions about allocating your time and energy. This will help you create a framework to balance personal and professional commitments while leaving room for love.

Effective time management is key. Learn to be organized and efficient in your work, maximizing productivity and minimizing wasted time. Utilizing calendars, to-do lists, and prioritization techniques can help you create a schedule that accommodates work and personal time. This will enable you to be present and fully engaged in your relationships without feeling overwhelmed by professional demands.

Communication is the cornerstone of maintaining balance and commitment in relationships. Openly discussing your commitments and aspirations with your loved ones, and seeking their understanding and support, can help create a collaborative approach to finding solutions when adjustments are needed. Remember that your loved ones are there to support you, and involving them in your journey not only eases the process but also strengthens your bond. Additionally, communication is key when it comes to sustaining commitment within a relationship. It's important to be open and honest with your partner, even when the conversation is uncomfortable or challenging. Address conflicts and concerns promptly and work together to find resolutions. Conflict is a natural part of any relationship, and how you navigate it is what truly matters. So, put on your communication cap, foster healthy discussions, and let the conversations flow, allowing your relationship to grow stronger through open dialogue.

Do not forget to take care of yourself. Self-care is crucial for maintaining balance and preventing burnout in the relationship with your special one. Carve out time for activities that rejuvenate and recharge you. Whether exercising, pursuing hobbies, or simply relaxing, self-care allows you to show up fully in your personal and professional life. Embrace flexibility and adaptability. Life is unpredictable, and unexpected relationship challenges or opportunities may arise. Be willing to adjust your plans and expectations as needed. Remember that balance is not a rigid state but a dynamic process that requires constant adjustment.

Finding balance is an ongoing practice. There will be times when work demands more of your attention and other times when personal commitments take precedence. It is about recognizing these shifts and making conscious choices to ensure love remains a cherished part of your life. So, my dear scholars, strive for balance by setting priorities, managing time effectively, communicating openly, practicing self-care, and embracing flexibility. Doing so allows you to navigate the beautiful choreography between personal and professional commitments while nurturing and cherishing the love that enriches your life.

Building a Foundation of Love.

First up, let's talk about laying down some solid groundwork. You wouldn't build a house on a shaky foundation, would you? Nope! The same goes for love. You have got to establish a strong emotional connection with your partner. That means really getting to know them—what makes them tick, what makes them laugh, what makes them ... well, them!

Now, trust, respect, and open communication. Oh boy, those are like the holy trinity of relationships! Without trust, you've got nothing but suspicion. Without respect, well, you're just asking for trouble. And as for communication? Well, let's just say it is the mortar that holds those relationship bricks together.

But wait, there's more! You've got to nurture those shared values and goals. Like the analogy shared earlier, nurturing is like tending to a garden—you've got to water it, give it some sunshine, and watch it bloom. When you and your partner are on the same page about where you're headed in life, magic happens. Trust me, I've seen it firsthand!

So, my fellow love architects, remember: Build that emotional foundation strong, keep those lines of communication open, and never forget to nurture those shared dreams. Your happily ever after? Well, it is waiting for you to lay down the bricks.

Commitment and Longevity.

Ah, commitment, the spark that keeps the flame of love burning bright! As I reflect on my marriage, I cannot help but emphasize the significance of commitment in a relationship. So, buckle up, and let's explore this topic together!

Commitment is like a sturdy ship sailing through the stormy seas of life. It is the unwavering dedication to your partner and the relationship you've built together. It means being there for each other through thick and thin and steadfastly weathering the ups and downs. Maintaining long-term commitment requires intentionality and effort. One strategy is to nurture and invest in your relationship continually. Like a plant needs water and sunlight, love needs care and attention.

As you strive to keep romance alive, life can sometimes feel like a whirlwind of responsibilities and obligations, but don't let that dampen the flame of love. Create shared experiences that bring you closer together. Inject some spontaneity and playfulness into your relationship. Make time for each other, create shared experiences, and keep the romance alive. Surprise your partner with a heartfelt gesture or a spontaneous date night. Trust me; it is worth the effort (and might earn you some extra brownie points, too!).

Challenges will inevitably arise, my dear graduates, but fear not! They are an opportunity for growth and greater connection. When faced with challenges, approach them as a team. Support each other, offer a listening ear, and be willing to compromise. And hey, don't forget to sprinkle a little humor along the way. Laughter is the best medicine, especially when faced with life's curveballs!

Naa Kleshie and I have encountered our fair share of challenges and conflicts. But through commitment, open communication, and a healthy dose of humor, we navigate those stormy waters and emerge stronger than ever. So, embrace commitment as the anchor that holds your relationship steady. Nurture your love, communicate openly, and face challenges together. Remember, commitment is not just a promise; it is a daily choice to choose love, even when the going gets tough. And trust me, the rewards of a long-lasting, fulfilling partnership are worth every ounce of effort!

As a new or recent graduate ready to start life, choosing the right life partner is one of the most important decisions you'll ever make. Here are some strategies that have worked for me to help you navigate this crucial choice and build a long-lasting relationship.

1. Role Models and Mentorship: Seek advice from couples who have been together for a long time and have a relationship you admire. Their insights can provide valuable guidance.

2. Premarital Counseling: Consider premarital counseling to discuss important topics and ensure you are on the same page before making a lifelong commitment.

3. Take Your Time: Don't rush the process. Take time to get to know your partner deeply before making major decisions.

Focusing on these strategies and being mindful of these significant aspects can build a strong foundation for a lasting and fulfilling relationship. Building a successful partnership takes effort, understanding, and a commitment to growing together.

Sustaining Quality Relationships.

Ah, my dear graduating seniors, welcome the wonderful world of sustaining quality relationships. As John Lennon passionately said, *"I'm not going to sacrifice love, real love, for any *%@$n' war or any friend, or any business because in the end, you're alone at night."* (John Lennon Quotes, n.d.). Love, oh sweet love, is the foundation upon which we build our lives. So, let's explore some essential aspects of sustaining a quality relationship.

First and foremost, continuous investment is the key. Love is money. Steep dough. Furthermore, it can be expensive. Just as a garden needs regular tending to flourish, with weeding, watering, and pruning, a relationship requires consistent care and maintenance. Make time for gardening your love - pulling out the weeds of resentment, nourishing it with quality time and affection, and carefully shaping it to grow in a healthy direction.

Love is a delicate flame that must be stoked regularly to stay strong and vibrant. You must tend to the fire, adding a new lagniappe of shared experiences and intimate moments, fanning the flames of passion, and protecting it from drafts that could snuff it out. Cultivating love is like baking a perfect soufflé – it demands patience, the right ingredients measured precisely, and a watchful eye to ensure it rises to glorious heights. You must carefully fold in trust, compromise, and open communication and resist the urge to peek before it is fully risen.

To truly know and understand your partner, make a habit of deep listening. Ask thoughtful questions beyond the superficial, and be present to hear their hopes, fears, and inner workings truly. Learn the intricate map of their emotional landscape and show them you have taken the time to memorize every path.

Celebrate small victories along the way, like you would the first blooms of spring or the first batch of perfectly baked cookies. Pause to appreciate the little moments that make your love special and unique. In doing so, you'll cultivate an abiding appreciation for each other that transcends the grand gestures. Celebrate milestones, big and small, and appreciate the unique qualities that make your partner special. Remember, love is a verb—it requires action!

Sustaining quality relationships requires a commitment to mutual support and understanding, especially for new graduates navigating their careers and personal lives. One effective and affordable way to encourage each other's personal growth is through regular check-ins. Setting aside time each week to discuss dreams and aspirations can foster an environment of trust and empowerment. Whether it's sharing goals over coffee or taking a walk in the park, these simple conversations can strengthen the bond between partners, ensuring that both individuals feel valued and inspired.

Another essential aspect of maintaining a strong relationship is finding budget-friendly ways to keep the romance alive. Graduates can prioritize activities that foster connection without breaking the bank. Planning home-cooked dinners, enjoying movie nights with favorite films, or exploring local parks together can create memorable experiences. Additionally, small gestures, like leaving thoughtful notes or surprising each other with a favorite snack, can reignite passion and reinforce the emotional connection that is vital for a healthy relationship.

Effective communication is also crucial for navigating challenges and celebrating successes together. New graduates should strive to create an open dialogue about feelings, expectations, and concerns, which can help prevent misunderstandings. Utilizing free resources such as relationship podcasts or online articles can provide valuable insights into improving communication skills. By prioritizing transparency and understanding, partners can build a resilient relationship that allows them to face challenges together while creating a shared future grounded in love and support.

Building a Solid Relationship and Career Success.

Imagine this scenario: you have work deadlines looming over you like dark clouds, but at home, your kids are demanding your attention like little tornadoes. How do you keep it all together without losing your mind? Well, let me share some wisdom from my 13 years of marital bliss.

Now, take a moment to reflect on the role of a supportive partner in career success. Behind every successful person is a cheerleader-in-chief, and mine happens to be my wonderful spouse. Having someone in your corner who believes in your dreams, lifts you when you're feeling down, and celebrates your victories as if they were their own is worth its weight in gold. A supportive partner helps you grow and achieve your personal and professional goals. Find someone who celebrates your successes, encourages your aspirations, and stands by you during tough times. Support and encouragement are critical to a fulfilling partnership.

But hey, it is not all rainbows and sunshine. Balancing family responsibilities with professional ambitions is like walking a tightrope over a pit of alligators. There will be days when you feel like you're spread thin and pulled in a million different directions. But fear not!

With a little bit of planning, a dash of flexibility, and a whole lot of love, you can have your cake and eat it, too.

So, in conclusion, remember this: building a solid family doesn't mean sacrificing your career ambitions, and vice versa. It is about finding that delicate dance between the two, with your partner by your side, cheering you on every step of the way. Trust me, it is a recipe for success in love and career.

Embracing Imperfections and Growth.

Finding true love isn't about seeking perfection, but about understanding that real relationships are built on acceptance and mutual growth. In a world that often glorifies perfection, it can be easy to overlook the beauty found in our flaws and the lessons learned through our struggles. Embracing imperfections is not just about accepting our shortcomings; it's about recognizing that these very flaws are integral to our growth and development. Each stumble, misstep, and moment of vulnerability offers invaluable insights that shape who we are and who we aspire to be. A fulfilling relationship is built not only on love but on accepting each other's flaws and nurturing the qualities that make the relationship truly beautiful. True love thrives when both individuals are willing to grow together, supporting each other through the highs and lows of life.

Encouraging personal and mutual growth is a vital ingredient in a fulfilling partnership. A strong relationship is not about stagnation. It is about embracing growth and supporting each other's aspirations. Encourage your partner to pursue their passions and dreams just as they should encourage you to chase yours. Cheer each other on, offering guidance and support along the way. Create an environment that celebrates personal growth, turning your dreams into reality.

Throughout our marriage, Naa Kleshie and I have learned the art of embracing imperfections and growing together. We've laughed at our quirks, forgiven each other's mistakes, and cheered for each other while pursuing personal and mutual growth. And let me tell you, it has made our bond stronger than ever.

Love as a Source of Strength.

Graduating seniors, let us delve into the incredible power of love as a source of strength in our lives. Being married has revealed strength to me that I never thought I had. I can attest to the profound impact love can have on our well-being. So, gather 'round as I share my stories and lessons learned from the journey of love.

Surround yourself with people that love you. Love possesses an incredible magic that fills us with strength and resilience. As Naa Kleshie and I poured our hearts and savings into the deeply personal pursuit of starting a family, we were humbled to discover the priceless gift of a truly kindred spirit who stood by our side. Though the financial toll was steep, the emotional support and unwavering understanding of this special someone buoyed us through the challenges and filled our souls with hope and joy that kept us going.

It is as if we have a superpower pulsing through our veins. Love gives us the bravery to confront life's challenges head-on, knowing that we have a partner ready to catch us if we stumble. It is like having a loyal sidekick on this grand adventure we call life. With their hand in ours, we face the unknown unafraid, secure in the knowledge that we are stronger together.

This profound connection transcends the day-to-day. It is a wellspring of courage that empowers us to take risks, chase our dreams, and weather any storm. No matter how dark the path ahead, the light of our love illuminates the way, guiding us onward. It is the ultimate superpower— a feeling and a transformative force that reshapes our reality. Together, our love turns obstacles into pathways, leading us to a future where anything is possible.

Love provides strength in times of difficulty, profoundly impacting our mental and emotional well-being. When enveloped in a warm, loving relationship, our hearts are lighter for our spirits to soar. Love brings joy, laughter, and a sense of belonging. It lifts and wraps us in a comforting embrace when we are feeling down and the world is overwhelming.

It is like having a personal cheerleading squad, always there to lift our spirits and remind us of our strength when self-doubt creeps in. With their unconditional encouragement, we face the unknown unafraid, secure in the knowledge that we are stronger together. And let's not forget the incredible power of overcoming challenges together. As previously mentioned, love isn't all sunshine and rainbows. There will be storms and obstacles along the way. But when you have a partner committed to weathering those storms with you, it's a game-changer. Together, you become a dynamic duo, ready to conquer any challenge that comes your way. And over the years, you'll look back on those challenges and realize they were the very moments that strengthened your bond and deepened your love.

The incredible power of love is a source of strength. Find someone who lifts you, brings you joy, and stands by your side. Together, you can overcome any challenge that life throws your way. Love truly is a superpower that can transform your life in the most extraordinary ways. Embrace and cherish love, letting it be the guiding light on your path to happiness and fulfillment.

Embracing Vulnerability and Trust.

The remarkable power of vulnerability and trust in cultivating a deep and lasting connection with your life partner is real. I continue to live it. I can assure you that both are the cornerstones of a strong and fulfilling relationship. Vulnerability unlocks the door to intimacy and strengthens the bond between partners. It is like unveiling your secret superhero identity and letting your partner see your true self. With vulnerability, you create a safe space where authenticity thrives. Walls crumble, masks fade, and you connect deeper, free from pretenses and facades. It is a beautiful dance of trust and openness that brings you closer than ever before.

Trust, cultivated through honesty, transparency, and reliability, is the foundation upon which vulnerability is built, like a delicate flower requiring nurturance and care. When you say you will be there, be there. When you make a promise, keep it. Trust is a two-way street, and it grows stronger when both partners consistently show up for each other. So, be a reliable source of support for trust to blossom, paving the way for vulnerability to flourish. A willingness to be open and share your fears, insecurities, and dreams with your partner is also a must and similar to baring your soul and saying, "Hey, this is me, with all my quirks and imperfections." Sharing your vulnerabilities creates a space for empathy, compassion, and understanding, strengthening your bond in ways you never thought possible. You will be amazed at how your partner responds with love and support, offering a comforting shoulder to lean on when life is most challenging and overwhelming.

My partner and I have learned the art of embracing vulnerability and trust. We've had our fair share of fears and insecurities but created a safe haven to share them without judgment. In those vulnerable moments, we have grown closer, understanding each other on a deeper level. We've built an unshakable foundation of trust through honesty, transparency, and reliability, and together, we've faced life's challenges head-on, knowing that we have each other's unwavering support.

So, as you embark on the path of choosing a life partner, remember the transformative power of embracing vulnerability and trust. Create a space where authenticity can thrive. In doing so, you'll forge a bond that can withstand the tests of time. Embrace vulnerability, cultivate trust, and embark on a journey of love and connection that will enrich your lives beyond measure.

Nurturing the Relationship.

Much like a thriving garden, relationships are like delicate flowers needing tender care and attention. Relationships thrive when we prioritize quality time, shared experiences, and meaningful gestures. It is like watering the garden of love, allowing it to flourish and bloom in all its glory. So, make it a point to carve out dedicated moments for each other, free from distractions and the hustle and bustle of life. Whether it is a romantic dinner date, a weekend getaway, or simply cuddling on the couch watching your favorite movie, these moments of togetherness nurture the bond between you and your partner.

But let's not forget the importance of keeping the spark alive. Relationships prosper with appreciation, affection, and gratitude. It is like adding a sprinkle of fairy dust that ignites the magic within your connection. Show appreciation for your partner's efforts, big or small, and let them know how much you value them. Shower them with affection, be it through a warm embrace, a sweet kiss, or a gentle touch. And never underestimate the power of gratitude—expressing your heartfelt thanks for the love and support your partner brings into your life. These simple acts of kindness and love create a ripple effect, keeping the flame of passion burning bright.

Partners can learn the art of nurturing their relationships through intentional effort and care. Every relationship experiences ups and downs, but prioritizing quality time together is essential for maintaining a strong bond. Whether through romantic getaways or unique adventures, creating cherished memories helps to deepen the connection between partners.

Additionally, showing appreciation and affection on a daily basis is vital. Simple gestures, such as leaving a handwritten note on the kitchen counter, preparing surprise breakfasts in bed, or having a spontaneous dance party in the living room, can significantly enhance emotional intimacy. These small acts of love and gratitude play a crucial role in keeping the relationship alive and flourishing.

When choosing a life partner, prioritize quality time, create shared experiences, and infuse your days with appreciation, affection, and gratitude. These simple but powerful acts will keep the spark alive and love growing stronger each day, nurturing your relationship like a cherished garden.

Balancing Individual Growth and Partnership.

Buckle up, folks! We're diving into one of the juiciest topics of all: balancing personal growth with being part of a dynamic duo. Trust me, after 13 years of marriage, I've got some tales to tell! First, encourage each other's personal and professional development. You know how they say, "Happy spouse, happy house"? Well, it's true! When you see your partner chasing their dreams, whether landing that dream job or finally mastering the art of making the perfect grilled cheese sandwich, you cannot help but feel proud. So, don't be shy—be their biggest cheerleader, their loudest supporter, and watch them soar!

Balancing independence and togetherness in a relationship is key to moving forward together while maintaining your own sense of self. Now, let's chat about finding that sweet spot between independence and togetherness. It's like riding a tandem bike, one bike with multiple riders. All riders have their own pedals but are going in the same direction, like maintaining your sense of self while part of a team. Take it from me- there's nothing more attractive than someone confident in who they are and still values being part of something bigger.

Planning for the Future.

Future planners and dreamers— let's talk about setting sail into the great unknown—your future! With all my marriage experience, I have learned that having a game plan can make all the difference in planning for a successful future.

First things first: discuss your vision for the future. It's like plotting a course on a treasure map—you've got to know where you are going! Talk about your dreams for your family, career, and lifestyle with your partner. Whether you envision owning a cozy cottage in the countryside or climbing the corporate ladder, ensure you are on the same page.

Second, create a shared vision and roadmap for your life together. It's like planning a cross-country road trip—sure, there may be detours and unexpected pit stops along the way, but having a map keeps you headed in the right direction. Work together to set goals, plan, and chart your course toward your shared dreams. But here's the kicker— be open to adapting and recalibrating your plans as you grow and evolve as a couple. Life has a funny way of throwing curveballs when you least expect it. So, stay flexible, stay nimble, and remember that sometimes, the best adventures are the ones you never saw coming.

Choosing a life partner is a decision of profound significance—one that shapes the trajectory of your life in myriad ways. By approaching this decision strategically, with a deep understanding of yourself and your values, you can cultivate a relationship that not only brings you joy and fulfillment but also serves as a source of strength and support on your journey toward personal and professional success. Remember, in the end, love sustains us through the trials of life, echoing John Lennon's timeless wisdom.

And there you have it! Choosing a life partner wisely and prioritizing love in your decision-making process is the glue holding everything together and the secret ingredient to personal and professional fulfillment.

As you venture into the great unknown, armed with new wisdom from my personal experience of marital bliss, I encourage you to choose your partner with care, nurture your relationship with love and laughter, and never forget that the greatest adventures are the ones you embark on together. So, here's to love, here's to life, and here's to all the incredible journeys that lie ahead. Cheers!

CHAPTER 9

Leaving the Nest for the Ideal Home Base

"It was a time before Facebook and Instagram and texting. I imagine it must be easier now for college students. Home must not feel so far away anymore. But how do you cut the apron strings if the strings are virtual?" (Kirstie Brote, n.d.).

Kirstie Collins Brote

Kirstie Collins Brote is the author of *Beware of Love in Technicolor,* a book featured on the social cataloging website *Goodreads.*

For today's graduating seniors and job seekers, the decision to leave home and find the best place to live is influenced by a myriad of tangible and intangible factors. As you stand at the threshold of adulthood, the choice of where to establish your new home is pivotal. It's not merely about finding a place to lay your head at night. It's about crafting a life that aligns with your aspirations, values, and career trajectory. Whether you're considering staying close to family, venturing out of state, or even contemplating an international move, each option comes with its own set of opportunities and challenges.

Whether you are drawn to the familiarity of home or the excitement of new beginnings, this chapter aims to support you as you embark on this transformative journey of leaving home and finding your place in the world. From navigating the emotional ties that bind you to your hometown to evaluating the practical considerations of different geographical locations, we'll delve into the complexities of this significant life transition. Each section provides insights, tips, and real-life anecdotes to help guide your decision-making and empower you to make the best choice for your unique circumstances.

Historically, the concept of *home* has transformed. The evolution of technology has redefined not only how we connect but also how we perceive and experience significant life transitions. Kirstie Collins Brote aptly observed, "It was a time before Facebook and Instagram and texting. I imagine it must be easier now for college students. Home must not feel so far away anymore. But how do you cut the apron strings if the strings are virtual?" (Kirstie Collins Brote, n.d.). This quote describes how the experience of leaving home and going to college has changed with modern technology and social media. The core idea is that modern technological connectivity has changed the college experience, making the separation from home a less severe experience and potentially making it more difficult for students to embrace their newfound independence fully.

Indeed, technology has blurred the lines between physical distance and emotional closeness. This implies that the best settling and thriving decisions require proper information to ensure satisfaction (Gati & Kulcsár, 2021).

As you stand at the threshold of adulthood, the choice of where to establish your new home is pivotal. It is not merely about finding a place to lay your head at night; it is about crafting a life that aligns with your aspirations, values, and career trajectory (Lehu, 2014). Whether you're considering staying close to family, venturing out of state, or even contemplating an international move, each option has its own set of opportunities and challenges.

Transitioning from the comforts of home to establishing an independent living situation is a significant milestone for many individuals. This journey often begins with the choice of cohabiting with roommates, which can offer both companionship and financial benefits. Successful coexistence requires clear communication and mutual respect. Setting ground rules about shared responsibilities, such as cleaning schedules and bill payments, can help prevent misunderstandings and foster a harmonious living environment. Regular check-ins can also facilitate open discussions about any concerns or adjustments needed, ensuring that everyone feels valued and heard.

Money management becomes a crucial skill when living independently for the first time. New occupants must learn to budget effectively, balancing income against expenses such as rent, utilities, and groceries. Creating a monthly budget can help individuals track their spending and identify areas where they can cut costs. It's also essential to build an emergency fund for unexpected expenses, providing a safety net that can alleviate financial stress. Learning to cook simple, budget-friendly meals can further enhance financial stability while promoting healthier eating habits.

The Emotions: Navigating Emotional Ties to Home.

Leaving home for the first time can evoke excitement and apprehension. When I departed from my home country, Ghana, and was bound for college in the United States of America, the experience felt like a scene from a captivating TV drama. My journey led me to New York, where I began my undergraduate studies at a mid-sized college in Pennsylvania.

Stepping off the plane at JFK Airport, I was greeted by an icy chill, unlike anything I had ever felt. Despite my preparations, I found myself unprepared for the biting cold. After a prolonged wait in the airport, my host family met me with a blended demeanor of concern and politeness. Determined to adapt to my new reality, I embarked on the journey to Allentown, navigating through snow-covered roads and contemplating the opportunities that awaited me in this foreign land.

As an international F-1 student, my early days in America were characterized by a rapid assimilation into a new way of life. Every moment seemed to blur the lines between dreams and reality, demanding my immediate attention, academically and personally. Amidst the whirlwind of adjustment, I discovered the importance of maintaining connections with loved ones back home while embracing the opportunities for growth in my new environment. It became clear that balancing cherished familiarity and exciting new experiences was essential for my personal development.

In times of homesickness, reaching out to family and friends proved to be a source of comfort, bridging the distance between continents with heartfelt conversations and virtual connections. However, equally important was the exploration of my new surroundings, diving into the local community, and forging new relationships. By immersing myself in unfamiliar settings, I cultivated a support system that helped me navigate the challenges of acclimating to life in a foreign land. Embracing the old and the new became my mantra, guiding me through the highs and lows of this transformative journey.

Living Close to Family: The Comforts and Challenges.

Living close to family has its pros and cons—it's a mix of comfort and challenge that can be both reassuring and restrictive. On one hand, being near loved ones provides a strong sense of security, offering support that helps you navigate life's ups and downs. However, this closeness can also feel confining, as if you're stuck in their shadow and unable to fully establish your own independence. The lines between your life and theirs can blur, making it difficult to create a space that's truly your own.

I remember the transition vividly – moving from the warm cocoon of my guest family's home in Allentown, Pennsylvania, to the blank canvas of a dorm room, bereft of family. At first, the isolation was jarring, like being cast adrift on the open sea. But as I began to plant my flag and shape my environment, I discovered the empowering freedom in that solitude.

Setting boundaries and cultivating your domain are crucial steps in maintaining your independence while still basking in the glow of your loved ones' presence. Remember, this is your life to craft – your dreams to pursue, your path to forge. You can nurture that delicate balance with careful tending, allowing their support to lift you up without ever feeling smothered. The key is to embrace the comfort of family while still blazing your trail, answerable to none but yourself. It's a delicate dance, to be sure, but one that holds the promise of a fully and authentically lived life.

The pull of family can be strong, offering a safety net full of practical benefits. When life gets tough, having family nearby—whether it is grandparents ready to babysit or relatives who can help with household repairs—can feel like a lifesaver. Their support during hard times is priceless.

However, it is important not to become too dependent on this support, as you also need to create your own life. As you work toward your goals and dreams, it is crucial to assert your independence while still maintaining those valuable family ties.

The key to finding this balance is open and honest communication. Share your goals with your family and express your need for independence. Let them offer advice, but also make it clear that you want to make your own choices. By doing this, you can keep a strong bond with your family while also building your own path.

It's a delicate balance—finding the right mix between relying on family and standing on your own. But when you achieve it, you'll enjoy both the security of your family's support and the excitement of creating your own future.

As the giddy thrill of commencement fades, a new reality sets in - the umbilical cord that once tethered you to home has suddenly grown taut, straining with the weight of physical and emotional distance. The family that has cradled you for so long now feels just out of reach; a support system that once seemed omnipresent is now accessible only through a screen.

Yet, in this newfound independence, there lies a wealth of opportunity. The practical advantages of proximity - from free home-cooked meals to a cadre of eager, available babysitters - are no longer a given. In their absence, you're faced with the daunting task of establishing your household, managing your finances, and carving out your space in the world.

It's a double-edged sword, this separation from the familiar. On one hand, losing that familial safety net can feel isolating, even terrifying. But on the other, it is the chance to prove your mettle, step into the fullness of your autonomy, and forge your own path. The key is to strike a delicate balance- to maintain that cherished bond with your loved ones while asserting your independence. Open and honest communication is essential, allowing you to share your dreams and ambitions without severing the ties that ground you. Carefully, you can nurture that support system even as you stretch your wings and take flight.

When considering where to live near your family, thorough research is essential. Treat the process with the same diligence as preparing for a final exam, compiling a comprehensive list of benefits and challenges. Consider local job opportunities, safety ratings, school districts, and community amenities. Don't hesitate to seek advice from family members who have experience with living in the area. And remember, there's no such thing as a dumb question when it comes to making such an important decision. Asking for guidance and clarification can help you make a more informed choice that aligns with your needs and preferences.

After all, this decision will shape the trajectory of your life in profound ways. Where you choose to plant your roots, build a home, and carve out a future will determine the opportunities available to you, the community that surrounds you, and the day-to-day rhythms that become the fabric of your existence. It is not a choice to be made lightly but rather one that deserves your complete attention and consideration.

Take the time to envision yourself in each potential location truly. Imagine the daily commute, the social circles, and the cultural offerings that will become an integral part of your life. This is not just a decision about real estate - it is a choice that will reverberate through every facet of your being, shaping the person you become and your life. Approach it with the gravity it deserves, and you'll be rewarded with a home that aligns with your values, aspirations, and vision for your future.

Venturing Out-of-State: Embracing New Horizons.

Imagine yourself in a brand-new state, surrounded by unfamiliar faces and places. It is a thrilling prospect, but it can also feel overwhelming. Take a deep breath and approach it one step at a time. Start by researching different areas, job markets, and the cost of living. Don't shy away from putting yourself out there and meeting new people. You never know what opportunities might await you when you step out of your comfort zone.

Moving to a new state offers more than just a change of scenery. It is a chance to start fresh and redefine yourself. Embrace the opportunity to immerse yourself in new cultures, cuisines, and ways of life. Remember, you're not just relocating to a different place. You're embarking on an adventure brimming with boundless possibilities.

After completing college, I ventured from Accra, Ghana, to cities across the United States, including Chicago, Illinois; Tustin, California; New Orleans, Louisiana; and eventually settled in Kennesaw, Georgia. Although the transition was far from smooth, each move was driven by the promise of career opportunities. I found myself taking on jobs outside my field of study simply to make ends meet, all while navigating the complex process of obtaining U.S. citizenship. Embracing these new horizons meant embracing the possibility of failure and using setbacks as progressions toward growth. Through these experiences, I learned valuable lessons and gained wisdom that guided me through subsequent challenges.

Each city presented its own set of opportunities and obstacles, with some lacking the familial support that I had grown accustomed to. The prospect of a vibrant, bustling metropolis held appeal, offering a wealth of career prospects and cultural stimulation. Yet, the thought of navigating that concrete jungle alone, without the comfort of familiar faces and helping hands, gave me pause. Smaller, quieter cities, on the other hand, exuded a sense of community and security that was undeniably tempting.

The chance to be surrounded by loved ones, to have a built-in support system at the ready, was a siren song that was hard to resist. However, the limited job opportunities and recreational options in these areas gave me reason to hesitate, concerned that I might feel stifled or unfulfilled.

Ultimately, I realized that there was no perfect solution, no city that could provide the ideal blend of professional potential and personal comfort. Each option came with its own set of trade-offs, requiring me to carefully weigh the priorities that mattered most. It was a decision that demanded deep introspection, a clear-eyed assessment of my values and long-term aspirations. Yet, precisely, these challenges fueled my determination and resilience, ultimately contributing to my success today. So, stay open-minded, embrace the journey of self-discovery, and remember that every challenge is an opportunity for personal growth.

Going Abroad: Expanding Your Global Perspective.

It is an exhilarating adventure, but it's not without hurdles. I have countless tales from my travels abroad, each offering unique insights into the complexities of life beyond borders. When you reside in your homeland, there's often little incentive to consider the perspectives of other cultures. The images you see on TV or online may seem idyllic, but they pale in comparison to the rich tapestry of experiences that await you abroad. Every sense is challenged as you confront language barriers, cultural nuances, and moments of homesickness. Yet, amidst the challenges, there's an opportunity for profound personal growth.

Navigating this new terrain requires a willingness to step outside your comfort zone. You'll find yourself questioning long-held assumptions, shedding preconceived notions, and embracing a more expansive worldview. Simple tasks like grocery shopping or ordering a meal can become immersive cultural lessons, sparking a deeper appreciation for the diverse ways people live their lives. And as you learn to adapt to these unfamiliar environments, you'll unlock a resilience and adaptability that will serve you well, no matter where your path may lead.

While living in another country broadens your horizons and reshapes your worldview, embrace the chance to immerse yourself in a new language, sample unfamiliar cuisines, and interact with people from diverse backgrounds. Being far from home can be daunting. However, the rewards of personal and professional development are immeasurable. View the challenges you experience as landmarks towards self-improvement, and never cease exploring the wonders of your new environment. The experiences you'll encounter abroad are unparalleled, offering invaluable lessons and perspectives that will shape you for years to come. My advice? Dive headfirst into the adventure, allow yourself to learn, appreciate, and emerge as a stronger, more enlightened individual.

Balancing Personal and Professional Goals.

Balancing personal and professional goals is akin to navigating a delicate tightrope. It's like juggling a troupe of circus performers, each demanding your undivided attention. One misstep and the whole carefully orchestrated act come crashing down. Maintaining this equilibrium is not unlike tending to an intricate garden, where you must prune and cultivate each bloom with equal care. Neglect the personal blossoms, and they wither; focus too intensely on the professional ones, and the whole ecosystem falls out of balance.

It requires introspection and courage to prioritize your happiness and fulfillment amidst the demands of career aspirations. Taking the time to reflect on your values and aspirations is crucial, allowing you to make decisions that align with your authentic self. From my experience, I've learned that tough decisions and bold moves are sometimes necessary to stay true to yourself. For instance, despite initial objections from my family, I stood firm in my personal choices, ultimately earning their respect and appreciation for my resilience and determination. Similarly, relocating from New Orleans to Georgia was a daunting leap, driven by the pursuit of better opportunities, yet it proved to be the right decision.

It's essential to recognize that each person's journey is uniquely theirs. While comparisons may arise, trust your instincts and embrace the risks that pave the way to success. As one of many siblings who shared similar educational opportunities, I've witnessed firsthand how divergent paths can lead to distinct destinations. Embracing these differences and having confidence in your capabilities is integral to forging a path toward personal and professional fulfillment.

Despite the challenges that may arise, embarking on the journey towards finding your ideal living situation and kickstarting your career is immensely rewarding. It's a journey of self-discovery and growth, where every obstacle and triumph contribute to your narrative. So, seize the opportunity to leave your mark on the world, unapologetically embracing the path that leads to your unique definition of success.

As we conclude this chapter, reflect on the profound changes in the landscape of transition for today's college graduates. Kirstie Collins Brote's observation about the impact of technology on the perception of home rings true. With the advent of social media and instant communication, the physical distance from home may seem less daunting, yet the emotional ties remain as strong as ever. In navigating this virtual proximity, recent graduates must grapple with the challenge of cutting apron strings now woven with digital threads.

Throughout this chapter, we've explored the myriad factors to consider when leaving the parental nest and establishing oneself in a new environment. Whether choosing to live close to family for support and familiarity, venturing out-of-state for new opportunities, or even daring to live abroad for a global perspective, each option presents its opportunities and challenges. From emotional ties to practical considerations, recent graduates must weigh their aspirations against the realities of their chosen path.

Ultimately, the journey of leaving home and finding the best place to live is one of self-discovery, resilience, and growth. It is about embracing new experiences, forging meaningful connections, and charting a course toward personal and professional fulfillment. Graduating from college marks the beginning of a new chapter where challenges and opportunities abound. Recent graduates can shape their destinies, whether navigating cultural adaptation, overcoming fear. or finding the courage to pursue one's dreams despite family expectations.

As you embark on this transformative journey, remember to trust yourself, follow your instincts, and embrace the challenges that come your way. Your path may not always be clear, but each step forward brings you closer to discovering your true home and realizing your full potential in your chosen career. So, go forth with confidence, knowing that the best place to live is not just a location on a map, but a state of mind where you find balance, fulfillment, and a sense of belonging.

CHAPTER 10

Use your migrant stories to your advantage

"Travel isn't always pretty. It isn't always comfortable. Sometimes it hurts, it even breaks your heart. But that's okay. The journey changes you; it should change you. It leaves marks on your memory, on your consciousness, on your heart, and on your body. You take something with you. Hopefully, you leave something good behind." (Anthony Bourdain, n.d.).

Anthony Bourdain

Anthony Bourdain was an American celebrity chef, author, and travel documentarian.

In the words of the late Anthony Bourdain, "Travel isn't always pretty. It isn't always comfortable. Sometimes, it hurts; it even breaks your heart. But that's okay. The journey changes you; it should change you. It leaves marks on your memory, on your consciousness, on your heart, and on your body. You take something with you. Hopefully, you leave something good behind." (Anthony Bourdain, n.d.). This sentiment resonates deeply with recent graduates and job seekers venturing into new career fields, particularly in North America and Europe.

As you navigate your professional path, understanding the significance of your migrant experiences can profoundly impact your journey. While embarking on your professional journey, it is essential to recognize the value of your migrant stories. Your experiences, struggles, and triumphs shape not only who you are but your approach to opportunities in the professional world. This chapter explores how you can leverage your migrant background to your advantage, transforming your unique narrative into a powerful asset in your career pursuits.

Embracing Cultural Diversity.

You know, diversity isn't just about the color of your skin or where you come from. It is about embracing the unique perspectives and experiences each person brings to the table. When stepping into the professional world, you encounter people from all walks of life, each with their own stories. Embrace the diversity of these new encounters with open arms. Take time to listen to others' perspectives. Ask questions, engage in conversations, and show genuine interest in getting to know your colleagues. Learn from their experiences, including their diverse cultures, traditions, and customs. Seek understanding.

Despite our differences, we often find commonalities in the similarities connecting us. Find common ground. Shared interests or values can serve as a foundation for building relationships with people from diverse backgrounds. Lead by example. Be an advocate for diversity and inclusion in your workplace. Challenge stereotypes, promote cross-cultural understanding, and champion initiatives that foster a sense of belonging for everyone. And, better yet, celebrate the richness of different cultures colliding.

When I started working in a 100% commission-based company, I was amazed by our team's cultural diversity. Instead of feeling intimidated, I embraced the opportunity to learn from my colleagues' diverse perspectives. This knowledge enriched my professional experience and helped me develop a deeper appreciation for the beauty of cultural diversity.

Navigating Cultural Communication Styles.

Navigating cultural nuances in the workplace can feel like learning a new language. It takes time, practice, and patience. From subtle differences in communication styles to varying expectations around hierarchy and decision-making, understanding these nuances is key to building effective relationships and thriving in diverse environments. Remember, it is not about conforming to a particular culture but rather about respecting and adapting to different ways of doing things.

Observe and adapt to your environment and team. Pay attention to how your colleagues communicate, make decisions, and interact with one another. Adapt your interactive approach accordingly to ensure clear communication and harmonious collaboration. Ask for clarification. Try not to assume or hesitate when clarification is needed, especially if you're unsure about cultural norms or expectations. People usually understand and appreciate the effort to learn and adapt. Be flexible. Cultivate a mindset of flexibility and openness to new ideas and perspectives. Embrace the opportunity to learn from cultural differences and incorporate them into your way of working. Many Americans like to lend a hand, especially to people who weren't born here.

Early in my career, I mistakenly assumed that everyone preferred indirect communication and consensus-building in decision-making. However, I quickly learned that in many American cultures throughout many states, direct communication and assertiveness are valued more highly. By adapting my communication style and approach, I was able to foster stronger relationships and achieve better outcomes in cross-cultural collaborations.

Leveraging Language Skills.

Your ability to speak multiple languages is an asset that can open doors and create opportunities in the professional world. Highlight your language skills. Prominently feature your language skills on your resume and online professional social media profiles. Incorporate specific details about your proficiency level and any relevant certifications or experiences.

Be proactive in offering your language skills to help colleagues or teams who may benefit from translation or interpretation services. Your language skills showcase your abilities and demonstrate your willingness to contribute to the team's success. Continue learning. Languages constantly evolve, so commit to honing your language skills through classes, immersion experiences, or self-study. The more fluent you become, the more doors will open in your career journey.

Building Global Networks.

Building global networks is essential for success in your professional career. Whether through social media platforms, professional associations, or industry conferences, actively seeking out opportunities to connect with professionals across the globe leads to new collaborations, mentorship opportunities, and career advancements. Remember, your network is your net worth, so invest time and effort into cultivating meaningful relationships with individuals who can support and inspire your career journey.

Utilize premier social media platforms to provide a powerful tool for expanding your professional network. Regularly engage with industry leaders, share relevant content, and participate in online discussions to increase visibility and connect with like-minded professionals. Attend networking events. Make it a priority to attend industry conferences, workshops, and networking events, both locally and internationally. These events provide valuable opportunities to meet new people, exchange ideas, and stay updated on industry trends. Follow up. After making new connections, follow up with personalized messages or invitations to connect further. Building rapport and nurturing relationships over time is key to maintaining a strong professional network.

Early in my career, I attended a conference where I had the opportunity to meet professionals from diverse backgrounds and industries. When I actively engaged in conversations, exchanged contact information, and followed up on those contacts, I expanded my network significantly. Over time, these connections proved invaluable, opening doors to new job opportunities, mentorship possibilities, and collaborative projects that enriched my professional journey.

Showcasing Adaptability.

In our rapidly changing work environment, adaptability is a crucial skill that can set you apart from your peers. Whether navigating organizational changes, embracing new technologies, or adjusting to different cultural norms, demonstrating your ability to adapt and thrive in diverse situations is essential for long-term success.

Embrace change as an opportunity for growth and innovation instead of meeting change with resistance. Approach new challenges with an open mind, a positive attitude, and a willingness to learn and adapt your approach as needed. Develop a mindset of agility and flexibility, allowing you to pivot and adjust to circumstances. Be proactive in seeking new learning opportunities and acquiring new skills to enhance your adaptability. Seek to receive feedback by soliciting feedback from colleagues, mentors, and supervisors to identify areas where you can improve and adapt your approach. Use this feedback as an opportunity for self-reflection and growth.

Throughout my career, I've encountered numerous challenges and obstacles requiring me to adapt and evolve. Whether learning to navigate a new organizational structure or adjusting to a different work culture, I approached each situation with openness, flexibility, resilience, and determination.

Did I have to put my pride aside when first learning to receive feedback? Oh, how that wounded my ego at times. I can still vividly remember the sharp sting of criticism, the knee-jerk defensiveness that would flare up, making me want to lash out or withdraw entirely. Our pride is such a fragile, fiercely guarded thing, isn't it? We cling to it so tightly, terrified that any chink in that armor will leave us exposed and vulnerable.

And I know I'm not alone in that struggle. So many of us immediately interpret feedback as an attack, an indictment of our capabilities and our worth. We bristle at the mere suggestion that our work, our ideas, and our very selves might be anything less than perfect. It is as if we've been programmed to see any critique as a personal slight, a judgment that cuts to the core of who we are. But we must realize that this mindset is holding us back. Feedback, when given with care and good intentions, is a gift - a chance to grow, to improve, to reach new heights. It is not about tearing us down but lifting us up. And the moment we can approach it with that mentality, with a genuine openness and humility, that's when the real magic starts to happen.

Because true adaptability, isn't about burying our pride. It is about having the courage to confront it, to acknowledge our flaws and shortcomings without letting them define us. It is about using that information, that outside perspective, to evolve and refine - not out of ego but out of a deep commitment to being the best version of ourselves. And believe me, that journey isn't always easy. But the payoff, the personal growth that comes from it, is more than worth it.

So, I urge you, my fellow graduates, to take a long, hard look at how you receive feedback. Challenge that knee-jerk defensiveness, that instinct to lash out. Instead, breathe deeply, open your mind and heart, and see the opportunity that lies within. It is not about losing your sense of self — it is about expanding, polishing, and turning it into something even stronger and more brilliant. And when you can do that, when you can truly embrace the gift of adaptability, the possibilities that unfold before you are truly limitless.

Communicating Transferable Skills.

Your experiences as a recent graduate and job seeker have equipped you with a unique and valuable set of transferable skills in the professional world. From problem-solving and critical thinking to communication and teamwork, effectively communicating these skills to potential employers is essential. Highlighting how your international experiences also shape your professional capabilities, setting you apart from other candidates and demonstrating your readiness to excel in diverse work environments.

Identify and inventory the transferable skills you've developed through academic studies, internships, volunteer work, and personal experiences. Focus on skills relevant to the positions you're applying for and highlight them in your resume and cover letter. When discussing your transferable skills in interviews or networking conversations, provide specific examples of how you've applied these skills in real-world situations. Use anecdotes or case studies to illustrate your capabilities and demonstrate your ability to deliver results. Tailor your messaging by customizing your communication to resonate with the needs and priorities of each prospective employer. Show how your transferable skills align with their organizational goals and how you can contribute to their success.

When individuals land their first big job interview after graduation, it is common to feel a surge of nerves. The culmination of years of hard work, sacrifice, and personal growth can feel overwhelming to convey in just a 30-minute conversation. However, reflecting on invaluable lessons learned during study abroad experiences can provide a solid starting point.

Challenges faced while living in a foreign country often test problem-solving skills. The language barrier, cultural differences, and unexpected obstacles can be daunting but also serve as opportunities to tap into creativity and resourcefulness. Sharing such experiences in an interview can captivate the interviewer, revealing the candidate's ability to think on their feet and navigate unfamiliar situations.

This ability to find solutions demonstrates transferable skills like adaptability, critical thinking, and composure under pressure. These qualities are not easily taught in a classroom; rather, they are developed through real-world experiences and set candidates apart in a competitive job market.

So, when you walk out of that interview, job offer in hand, you will know that it wasn't just your academic credentials that sealed the deal. The rich tapestry of your life experiences, the lessons you had learned beyond the bounds of campus, truly made the difference. And that is the power of effectively communicating your transferable skills. Because the truth is, the world beyond the ivory tower is complex, unpredictable, and ever-changing. Employers aren't just looking for graduates; they're seeking adaptable, resilient problem-solvers who can thrive in the face of adversity. And if you can showcase those invaluable qualities, drawn from the full breadth of your experiences, then you'll have a distinct advantage in standing out from the crowd.

As you proceed to the next chapter, I urge you to embrace the lessons you've learned and the skills you've honed inside and outside the classroom. Don't be afraid to share your stories, to highlight the ways in which you've grown and evolved. Because those unique experiences, those moments of challenge and triumph, are what makes you succeed.

Overcoming Stereotypes.

As a former nonimmigrant graduate and job seeker, I know all too well the frustration and self-doubt that can come from facing stereotypes and biases. When you're just starting out in your career, it can feel like an uphill battle, with preconceived notions about your background and abilities standing in the way of the opportunities you've worked so hard to earn. But let me tell you, the key is to not let those stereotypes define you. Don't let them undermine the confidence you've built, the skills you've honed, the unique experiences that make you who you are. Instead, use that as fuel to prove to yourself your strengths, to challenge unfounded assumptions, and to show the world just how capable and talented you truly are.

There was a time when skepticism emerged from a few colleagues who questioned my abilities based solely on my foreign accent. It was disheartening to have hard work and dedication undermined by unfounded perceptions. However, the response was to embrace the accent as a part of identity while focusing on delivering high-quality work. By consistently producing excellent results and actively seeking opportunities to demonstrate skills, respect was earned from peers through professionalism and dedication. Managing a foreign accent in the workplace became an opportunity to showcase resilience and commitment, proving that expertise transcends language barriers.

And let me tell you, the feeling of watching those preconceived notions crumble, of seeing the shift in my colleagues' attitudes as they realized just how wrong they had been - it was immensely gratifying. Because that's the power of leading by example, of using your actions to defy stereotypes and prove your worth. It is not about confrontation or retaliation; it is about consistently demonstrating your competence, your value, and your unwavering commitment to being the best version of yourself.

Now, I know it's not always easy. There will be setbacks. There will be moments of frustration where you feel like the odds are stacked against you. But that's where the importance of surrounding yourself with mentors, allies, and advocates comes into play. Lean on those individuals, draw strength from their guidance and support, and let them remind you of your incredible potential.

Because the truth is, you are so much more than any stereotype or bias that might try to hold you back. You are the product of your unique experiences, your hard-won accomplishments, your relentless pursuit of growth and excellence. And when you channel that energy and let it shine through in everything you do, you'll be unstoppable.

Take a deep breath, hold your head high, and go out there and show the world what you're made of. Lead by example and demonstrate your competence and professionalism through your actions and behaviors. Show up prepared, meet deadlines, and exceed expectations to earn the respect of your colleagues and supervisors. Educate others about your background and experiences, dispelling myths and misconceptions.

In the words of Anthony Bourdain, "*Travel isn't always pretty. It isn't always comfortable. Sometimes it hurts, it even breaks your heart. But that's okay.*" And you know what? The same can be said for the path I chose as a non-immigrant graduate. It hasn't always been easy, has it? The doubts, the setbacks, the moments where you feel like the odds are stacked against you – they can be truly gut-wrenching. But here's the thing: those challenges, those hardships, they are what shape us. They leave indelible marks on our memories, our consciousness, our hearts, and our very beings. And while it may not feel like it at the moment, those

358

experiences, those migrant stories, are not just tales of struggle – they are powerful narratives of resilience, adaptation, and growth.

This chapter explored countless insights, tips, and anecdotes to help us leverage our unique backgrounds. From embracing cultural diversity to showcasing our adaptability and overcoming stereotypes, we now have the tools and resources to thrive in even the most diverse work environments. And you know what? We should be damn proud of that.

As we move forward, we must continue to tell our migrant stories with a sense of pride and unwavering confidence. Because those experiences aren't just burdens to bear – they are lenses through which we view the world, sources of inspiration for ourselves and others. They have shaped us into the resilient, adaptable, and culturally competent individuals we are today, and they will continue to guide us as we navigate our professional careers.

CHAPTER 11

Conclusion: Conquering the Unexpected

"One of the greatest discoveries a man makes, one of his great surprises, is to find he can do what he was afraid he couldn't do." (Henry Ford Quotes, n.d.).

Henry Ford

Henry Ford was an American industrialist and business magnate, founder of the Ford Motor Company, and sponsor of the development of the mass production assembly line technique with a net worth of $200 billion (in 2018 dollars; inflation-adjusted)

Navigating the Unexpected.

In life, especially as graduating seniors step into professional careers, we often face a whirlwind of uncertainty and apprehension. Yet, within this very precipice of time, we uncover our greatest potential and surprising capabilities. As Henry Ford astutely observed, *"One of the greatest discoveries a man makes, one of his great surprises, is to find he can do what he was afraid he couldn't do."* (Henry Ford Quotes, n.d.). This sentiment encapsulates the essence of our final chapter, aptly titled *Conclusion: Conquering the Unexpected.*

Throughout this book, we have explored various aspects of transitioning from the college world to the workforce, each chapter offering insights and guidance on navigating the challenges and seizing the opportunities that come our way. As we reach the peak of our adventure, let us raise a toast to the unpredictability of this journey and the resilience it develops within us.

Reflecting on the Journey.

As you reflect on your journey from eager student to budding professional, recognize the growth and transformation you've undergone. Remember when you first stepped into the real world, uncertain and overwhelmed? That's completely normal! Like you, many have navigated these waters before, and they've come out stronger on the other side. Use this moment to appreciate how far you've come and the hurdles you've overcome. Each experience, whether positive or challenging, has shaped you into the capable person you are today.

Embracing Fear and Uncertainty.

One of the most valuable lessons I've learned along my own journey is the importance of embracing fear and uncertainty. It's natural to feel uneasy about the unknown, but it is also where some of our greatest opportunities lie. Think back to a time when you faced a scary task or took a leap of faith into uncharted territory. Despite your initial hesitation, you likely discovered newfound strengths and capabilities you never knew you had. Embracing fear doesn't mean ignoring it. It means acknowledging it and pushing past it to reach your full potential. Feelings about fear and uncertainty are like roadblocks on your journey, but they don't have to stop you in your tracks. They can be opportunities for growth and discovery. You may have felt scared or unsure of yourself but pushed through those feelings and took a chance. And guess what? You succeeded! That's the power of embracing fear and uncertainty – it opens doors you never knew existed.

I remember being fresh out of college and unsure of the future. I was terrified of failing, of not living up to expectations. But then I realized something profound: failure is not the end. It's just a step on the path to success. Every setback taught me something valuable, whether it was resilience, perseverance, or simply the importance of humility. So don't let fear hold you back.

Instead, use it as fuel to propel you forward toward your goals.

As you navigate the ups and downs of your career, remember that it's okay to feel scared or uncertain at times. It's completely normal! The key is not to let those feelings paralyze you. Take a deep breath, remind yourself of your strengths, and forge ahead with confidence. You'll be amazed at what you can accomplish when you refuse to let fear dictate your actions. So, embrace the unknown, embrace the challenges, and embrace the opportunities that lie ahead. You can handle it.

Celebrating Personal Growth.

Now, let's take a moment to celebrate how much you've grown. From your first day of college to now, you've come a long way. Think about all the skills you've acquired, the obstacles you've overcome, and the person you've become. It's truly something to be proud of! Remember, growth doesn't happen overnight.

It's a journey filled with ups and downs, twists and turns. But through it all, you've remained resilient and determined. That sets you apart.

I will let you in on a little secret: personal growth is not just about achieving your goals. It is about becoming the best version of yourself. It is about pushing past your comfort zone, taking risks, and learning from your experiences. So, do not be afraid to challenge yourself and embrace new opportunities. Whether tackling a challenging project at work or volunteering for a leadership role, each step brings you closer to reaching your full potential.

As you reflect on your personal growth, remember to celebrate your successes, no matter how small. Whether mastering a new skill or overcoming a difficult obstacle, each achievement is a testament to your hard work and determination. So, take a moment to acknowledge how far you've come. And don't forget to keep pushing yourself to new heights because the journey of personal growth is never truly complete.

Embracing Failure as a Stepping Stone.

Failure is a word that often carries a negative connotation, but it is an essential part of learning. Think back to a time when you experienced failure. Maybe you didn't get the job, or your project didn't go as planned. It is easy to feel discouraged in those moments, but I want you to remember this: failure is not the end; it's just a detour on the road to success. Every setback is an opportunity to learn and grow, reassess your approach, and come back even stronger.

Early in many careers, professionals may encounter major setbacks that lead them to question their abilities and future prospects. After investing significant effort into a project, it can be disheartening when it falls apart at the last moment. This experience often brings feelings of disappointment and the temptation to give up. However, it is important to recognize that failure does not define a person's worth; rather, it serves as valuable feedback on their efforts.

With this perspective, people can regroup, learn from their experiences, and move forward. By applying the lessons learned from past failures, they can approach new challenges with renewed determination. In many cases, the next project may turn out to be a success, demonstrating the growth that comes from overcoming obstacles.

So, the next time you experience failure, don't let it define you. Instead, use it as a springboard for growth and innovation. Ask yourself what went wrong and what you can do differently next time. And remember, failure is not the opposite of success. It's a stepping stone on the path to success. So, embrace it, learn from it, and keep moving forward. You've got this!

Finding Resilience in Adversity.

Resilience is the ability to bounce back from adversity, stronger than before. Throughout your career, you will certainly face challenges and setbacks. But understand that how you respond to obstacles defines your success. Think back to a time when you encountered a roadblock. Maybe you didn't get the promotion you were hoping for, or you faced criticism from a colleague. It's natural to feel discouraged in these moments, but I want to remind you that setbacks are not the end of the road. They are just detours on the path to success.

I've faced my fair share of career challenges, and each one has taught me valuable lessons about resilience. One of the most important lessons I've learned is the power of perseverance. When faced with adversity, it's easy to throw in the towel and walk away, but true resilience means pushing through tough times to come out stronger on the other side. So, the next time you encounter a setback, don't let it defeat you. Instead, dig deep, tap into your inner strength, and keep moving forward. You'll be amazed at your capabilities when you refuse to give up.

Another aspect of resilience is maintaining a positive mindset. It's easy to dwell on the negative and succumb to self-doubt, but remember, every setback is an opportunity for growth. Instead of focusing on what went wrong, reflect on what you can learn from the experience and how you can use it to propel forward. By maintaining a positive attitude and a growth mindset, you will weather the storms of adversity and emerge stronger and more resilient than ever before. Keep your chin up, graduate, and remember that you have the power to overcome any obstacle that comes your way.

Cultivating a Growth Mindset.

In your journey from student to professional, your mindset will play a crucial role in shaping your experiences and outcomes. A growth mindset is about believing in your ability to learn and grow, even during challenges. Think back to when you encountered a difficult task. Maybe it was mastering a new skill or tackling a complex project. Instead of viewing it as an insurmountable obstacle, approach it with a growth mindset, knowing that with effort and perseverance, you can and will overcome any challenge that comes your way.

I've always believed that mindset is everything. I've encountered countless challenges and setbacks throughout my career, but my belief in the power of growth and learning has propelled me forward. Instead of viewing failure as a reflection of my abilities, I see it as an opportunity for improvement. By cultivating a growth mindset, I've turned setbacks into bridges, obstacles into opportunities, and challenges into triumphs.

So, how can you cultivate a growth mindset in your own life? It starts with embracing challenges and viewing them as opportunities for growth. Instead of fearing failure, see it as a natural part of the learning process. Surround yourself with people who inspire and encourage you, and don't be afraid to seek feedback and constructive criticism. Remember, the journey to success is not always easy, but with a growth mindset, you can overcome any obstacle that stands in your way. Embrace the journey, the challenges, and the growth that comes with it.

Paying It Forward.

As you navigate your career journey and experience success along the way, it is essential to remember those who helped you get to where you are today. Think back to the mentors, teachers, colleagues, and supportive family members who supported and encouraged you when times were tough. Their guidance and wisdom played a crucial role in shaping your path, and now it's your turn to pass that support on to others.

I've always believed that success is not just about achieving your goals. Instead, it's about lifting others along the way. Throughout my career, I've been fortunate to have mentors who believed in me and invested their time and energy into helping me succeed. And now, I pay it forward by mentoring others and offering support and guidance. Whether sharing insights from my experiences or offering a listening ear to someone going through a tough time, I believe we all have a responsibility to give back and support the next generation of professionals.

If you want to join me in giving back, consider joining my foundation, *The Adoo Family Foundation* as one of many options. I can't think of a more meaningful way to pay it forward than getting involved with an organization like this. Whether volunteering your time, sharing your expertise as a mentor, or making a financial contribution, every bit of support can make a profound difference in the lives of these deserving students. And in doing so, you'll not only be changing their trajectories – you'll be investing in a future where talented, but hardworking individuals from all backgrounds also have the opportunity to thrive.

So, how can you pay it forward in your career journey? It starts with being generous with your time and knowledge. Take the time to mentor someone just starting their career. Offer to share your expertise with a colleague who is struggling. Volunteer your time to support a cause you believe in. Remember, the impact you can have on someone else's life may far exceed your expectations, and the ripple effect of your kindness and generosity can create a positive change that extends far beyond your circle. So, graduate, pay it forward, and watch your actions inspire others to do the same.

Looking Ahead.

As you stand on the brink of new opportunities and adventures, it is essential to approach the future with optimism and enthusiasm. Think back to the goals and dreams you set for yourself when you first embarked on this journey. Now, imagine all the incredible possibilities ahead as you continue to grow and evolve in your career.

I've always believed that the best way to predict the future is to create it. In my career journey, I've learned that success is not a destination; it's a journey filled with twists and turns, ups and downs. But by staying focused on my goals and maintaining a positive outlook, I've been able to weather the storms and seize the opportunities that have come my way. So, as you look ahead to the future, remember that you have the power to shape your destiny.

How can you prepare for the future and set yourself up for success? It starts by setting clear goals and creating a plan to achieve them. Take the time to reflect on what you truly want from your life and career, and then take actionable steps to make those dreams a reality. Surround yourself with people who support and encourage you, and do not be afraid to take calculated risks and step out of your comfort zone. And most importantly, remember that the journey to success is not always easy. But with dedication, perseverance, and a positive attitude, you have the power to create a future that exceeds your wildest dreams.

As you embark on this next chapter of your journey, I want to leave you with one final piece of advice: embrace the unknown, challenges, and opportunities. The road ahead may be uncertain, but with courage and determination, you can navigate it with grace and confidence. So, here's to the future: graduate – may it be filled with endless possibilities and boundless opportunities for growth and success.

Achieving good grades on your transcript took hard work and is an impressive accomplishment you should be proud of. However, grades are just a tiny part of the equation. What do straight As signify if you can't enter your desired career field or fully showcase your skills and potential?

While this book provides insight into navigating the expectations of the workplace, either explicitly taught during college or not, I hope it serves as a guide to help you integrate all aspects of your experience— academic achievements, personal brand, and future aspirations—to not only enter your desired career but excel and flourish within it.

As we embark on the next chapter of our lives, let us carry the lessons learned, memories cherished, and friendships forged. Let us remember that this unpredictable world is not something to be feared but embraced. For it is within this chaos that our greatest discoveries await. So, here's to your journey and the endless possibilities ahead. Cheers!

REFERENCES

Aithal, P. S., & Kumar, P. M. (2016). Using six thinking hats as a tool for lateral thinking in organizational problem-solving. *International Journal of Engineering Research and Modern Education (IJERME)*, 1(2), 225-234.

Alsop, R. (2008). *The trophy kids grow up: How the millennial generation is shaking up the workplace*. John Wiley & Sons.

Anthony Bourdain Quotes. (n.d.). Goodreads.com. Retrieved June 26, 2024, from Goodreads.com Web site: https://www.goodreads.com/quotes/872000-travel-isn-t-always-pretty-it-isn-t-always-comfortable-sometimes-it

Bacalja, A., Beavis, C., & O'Brien, A. (2022). Shifting landscapes of digital literacy. *The Australian Journal of Language and Literacy*, 45(2), 253-263.

Baer, G. (2003). *Real love: The truth about finding unconditional love and fulfilling relationships*. Penguin.

Bendick, P. J. (2014). Learning never stops. *Journal of Diagnostic Medical Sonography, 30*(2), 51-51.

Bertelsen, K. (n.d.). *Soft skills: Success may depend on them*. Page One Economics. https://www.econlowdown.org/v3/public/soft-skills-success-may-depend-on-them#:~:text=Washington's%20words%20inspire%20you%20to,Wish%20They'd%20Learned%20Sooner

Black, P., & van den Broek, D. (2013). New beginnings: Tackling the problem of lookism and the role of dress for success. https://ses.library.usyd.edu.au/handle/2123/6341

Boyles, D., Carusi, T., & Attick, D. (2009). Historical and critical interpretations of social justice. In *Handbook of social justice in education* (pp. 30-42). Routledge.

Brady-Myerov, M. (2021). *Listen wise: Teach students to be better listeners*. John Wiley & Sons.

Brown, B. (2015). *Daring greatly: How the courage to be vulnerable transforms the way we live, love, parent, and lead*. Penguin.

Browne, J. (2019). *How to analyze people: The power of emotional intelligence*.

Carson, R. (2023). *The art of connection: Building strong and meaningful relationships in a digital age*. Amazon.com Services LLC.

Cary, M. (2017, September 20). *Hard cases: What happens when a medical mistake has an unthinkable outcome*. LinkedIn. https://www.linkedin.com/pulse/hard-cases-what-happens-when-medical-mistake-has-cary-md-mba-mph?trk=public_profile_article_view

Castillo De Mesa, J., Gómez Jacinto, L., López Peláez, A., & Palma García, M. D. L. O. (2019). Building relationships on social networking sites from a social work approach. *Journal of social work practice, 33*(2), 201-215.

Chapman, G. (2015). *The 5 love languages: The secret to love that lasts*. Northfield Publishing.

Cherry, K. (2023, March 22). How to be open-minded and why it matters. *Verywell Mind*. https://www.verywellmind.com/be-more-open-minded-4690673

Clark, D. (2014, June 19). *How to succeed in a cross-cultural workplace*. Forbes. Updated March 31, 2015. Retrieved from https://www.forbes.com/sites/dorieclark/2014/06/19/how-to-succeed-in-a-cross-cultural-workplace/

Cloninger, C. R., Przybeck, T. R., Svrakic, D. M., & Wetzel, R. D. (1994). The Temperament and Character Inventory (TCI): A guide to its development and use.

Cochrane, B. S., Ritchie, D., Lockhard, D., Picciano, G., King, J. A., & Nelson, B. (2019, May). A culture of compassion: How timeless principles of kindness and empathy become powerful tools for confronting today's most pressing

healthcare challenges. In *Healthcare Management Forum*

(Vol. 32, No. 3, pp. 120-127). Sage CA: Los Angeles, CA:

SAGE Publications.

Consumer Financial Protection Bureau [CFPB]. (n.d.).

https://www.consumerfinance.gov

de Bono, E. (1985). *Six thinking hats: An essential approach to business management*. Little, Brown, and Company.

De Garrido, L., Gómez Sanz, J. J., & Pavón Mestras, J. L. (2021).

Foundations for the design of a creative system based

on the analysis of the main techniques that stimulate

human creativity.

Deepa, S., & Seth, M. (2013). Do soft skills matter?-Implications

for educators based on recruiters' perspective. *IUP

Journal of Soft Skills, 7*(1), 7-20.

Demarin, V., & Derke, F. (2020). Creativity—the story continues: An overview of thoughts on creativity. *Mind and brain: Bridging neurology and psychiatry*, 1-20.

Deutschendorf, H. (2009). *The other kind of smart: Simple ways to boost your emotional intelligence for greater personal effectiveness and success.* HarperChristian+ ORM.

Duffy, J., & Feltovich, N. (2002). Do actions speak louder than words? An experimental comparison of observation and cheap talk. *Games and Economic Behavior, 39*(1), 1-27.

Erickson, R. J. (1995). The importance of authenticity for self and society. *Symbolic interaction, 18*(2), 121-144.

Erickson, S. (2021). Communication in a crisis and the importance of authenticity and transparency. *Journal of Library Administration, 61*(4), 476-483.

Erik Qualman Quotes. (n.d.). Goodreads.com. Retrieved July 1, 2024, from Goodreads.com Web site:

https://www.goodreads.com/author/quotes/2929393.Er
ik_Qualman

Estlund, C. (2010). Just the facts: the case for workplace
transparency. *Stan. L. Rev., 63,* 351.

Federal Student Aid [FSA]. (n.d.). https://studentaid.gov

Finley, A. P. (2021). *How College Contributes to Workforce
Success: Employer Views on What Matters Most.*
Washington, DC: Association of American Colleges and
Universities [AAC&U]. 27-29.

Finley, A. P. (2023). *The career ready graduate-What employers
say about the difference college makes.* Washington, DC:
Association of American Colleges and Universities
[AC&U]. 20-23. Retrieved from AAC&U-2023-Employer-
Report.pdf (dgmg81phhvh63.cloudfront.net).

Fishman, A. A. (2016). How generational differences will impact
America's aging workforce: Strategies for dealing with

aging Millennials, Generation X, and Baby Boomers. *Strategic HR Review, 15*(6), 250-257.

Foster, M. K. (2022). Embracing a growth mindset: An experiential exercise to explore beliefs about learning. *Management Teaching Review, 7*(2), 132-154.

Garner, J. (2017). *It's who you know: How a network of 12 key people can fast-track your success.* John Wiley & Sons.

Gati, I., & Kulcsár, V. (2021). Making better career decisions: From challenges to opportunities. *Journal of Vocational Behavior, 126,* 103545.

Gottman, J. M., & DeClaire, J. (2001). *The Relationship cure: A 5 step guide to strengthening your marriage, family, and friendships.* Random House.

Gottman, J. M., & Silver, N. (2015). *The seven principles for making marriage work.* Harmony.

Gibson, C., H. Hardy III, J., & Ronald Buckley, M. (2014).

   Understanding the role of networking in organizations.

   Career Development International, 19(2), 146-161.

Giles, S. (2016). The most important leadership competencies,

   according to leaders around the world. *Harvard Business

   Review Digital Articles,* 2–6.

Ginwright, S., Cammarota, J., & Noguera, P. (2005). Youth, social

   justice, and communities: Toward a theory of urban

   youth policy. *Social justice, 32*(3 (101), 24-40.

Global, D. Global Business Coalition for Education. (2018).

   *Preparing tomorrows workforce for the Fourth Industrial

   Revolution. For business: A framework for action.

   Disponible en Internet: https://www2. deloitte.

   com/content/dam/Deloitte/global/Documents/About-

   Deloitte/gx-preparing-tomorrow-workforce-for-4IR. pdf

   Consultado, 18,* 19.

Goleman, D. (2006). *Social intelligence: The new science of human relationships*. Bantam Books.

Gray, K. (2024, January 16). *Recruiters and students have differing perceptions of new grads' proficiency in competencies*. National Association of Colleges and Employers. Retrieved from https://www.naceweb.org/career-readiness/competencies/recruiters-and-students-have-differing-perceptions-of-new-grads-proficiency-in-competencies

Gupta, M., Uz, I., Esmaeilzadeh, P., Noboa, F., Mahrous, A. A., Kim, E., ... & Kulikova, I. (2018). Do cultural norms affect social network behavior inappropriateness? A global study. *Journal of Business Research*, *85*, 10-22.

Half, R. (2024, January 29). *Skills to put on a resume employers will actually read (with examples!)*. Robert Half. https://www.roberthalf.com/us/en/insights/landing-job/skills-that-will-make-your-resume-pop

Hamm, N. (2019, April 8). *11 soft skills healthcare executives need to succeed*. Managed Healthcare Executive. https://www.managedhealthcareexecutive.com/view/11 -soft-skills-healthcare-executives-need-succeed

Harris, C. A. (2014). Confident expectancy. *Network Journal, 21*(4), 44.

Hennessey, T. (2014). *Hunger strike : Margaret Thatcher's battle with the IRA, 1980-1981*. Irish Academic Press.

Henry Ford Quotes. (n.d.). *BrainyQuote.com*. Retrieved June 26, 2024, from BrainyQuote.com Web site: https://www.brainyquote.com/quotes/henry_ford_1337 53

Howe, N., & Strauss, W. (2000). *Millennials rising: The next great generation*. Vintage.

Ibarra, H., & Hunter, M. (2007). How leaders create and use networks. *Growth, 35*(1), 101-103.

iCIMS. (2017, August 28). *New research defines the soft skills that matter most to employers*. Matawan, NJ. Retrieved from https://www.icims.com/company/newsroom/new-research-defines-the-soft-skills-that-matter-most-to-employers/

John Lennon Quotes. (n.d.). Goodreads.com. Retrieved June 25, 2024, from Goodreads.com Web site: https://www.goodreads.com/quotes/345346-i-m-not-going-to-sacrifice-love-real-love-for-any

John, J. (2009). Study on the nature of impact of soft skills training programme on the soft skills development of management students. *Pacific Business Review*, 19-27.

Jorgic, D. (2016, August 13). Michelle Carter becomes first American woman to win gold in shot put. *Reuters*. https://www.huffpost.com/entry/michelle-carter-gold_n_57af91e0e4b069e7e50590d0

Kadakia, C. (2017). *The millennial myth: Transforming misunderstanding into workplace breakthroughs*. Berrett-Koehler Publishers.

Kahnweiler, J. (2015). *The genius of opposites: How introverts and extroverts achieve extraordinary results together*. Berrett-Koehler Publishers.

Kane, A., Yarker, J., & Lewis, R. (2021). Measuring self-confidence in workplace settings: A conceptual and methodological review of measures of self-confidence, self-efficacy and self-esteem. *International coaching psychology review, 16*(1), 67.

Kantrowitz, M. (2012). Who graduates college with six-figure student loan debt?. *Student Aid Policy Analysis*, 2.

Kaputa, C. (2016). *Graduate to a great career: How smart students, new graduates and young professionals can launch BRAND YOU*. Nicholas Brealey.

Kaushik, M., & Guleria, N. (2020). The impact of pandemic COVID-19 in workplace. *European Journal of Business and Management, 12*(15), 1-10.

Kavanagh, M. H., & Drennan, L. (2008). What skills and attributes does an accounting graduate need? Evidence from student perceptions and employer expectations. *Accounting & Finance, 48*(2), 279-300.

Kaye, B., & Giulioni, J. W. (2012). *Help them grow or watch them go: Career conversations employees want*. Berrett-Koehler Publishers.

Kirstie Collins Brote Quotes. (n.d.). Goodreads.com. Retrieved June 25, 2024, from Goodreads.com Web site: https://www.goodreads.com/quotes/834915-it-was-a-time-before-facebook-and-instagram-and-texting

Kleinke, C. L. (1986). Gaze and eye contact: a research review. *Psychological bulletin, 100*(1), 78.

Kowarski, I., & Wood, S. (2024, June 20). 44 graduate degree jobs that pay six-figure salaries. *U.S. News & World Report*. https://www.usnews.com/education/best-graduate-schools/articles/graduate-degree-jobs-that-pay-six-figure-salaries

Lampinen, A., McMillan, D., Brown, B., Faraj, Z., Cambazoglu, D. N., & Virtala, C. (2017, June). Friendly but not friends: Designing for spaces between friendship and unfamiliarity. In *Proceedings of the 8th International Conference on Communities and Technologies* (pp. 169-172).

Lara-Palma, A. M., Brotóns-Cano, R., Delgado-Hurtado, M. M., Jiménez, A., Valencia-García, O., & Jimeno-Bulnes, M. M. (2022). 21st century skills: What else?. In *ICERI2022 Proceedings* (pp. 8529-8536). IATED.

Lauryn Hill Quotes. (n.d.). BrainyQuote.com. Retrieved June 28, 2024, from BrainyQuote.com Web site:

https://www.brainyquote.com/quotes/lauryn_hill_32844 1

Lehu, P. A. (2014). *Living on your own: The complete guide to setting up your money, your space, and your life*. Quill Driver Books.

Litalien, B. C. (2012). *Towards a framework of the social franchise: A management construct for nonprofit leaders*. University of Maryland University College.

Looney, A. (2022). Student loan forgiveness is regressive whether measured by income, education, or wealth. *Hutchins Center Working Papers*.

Lynch, M. (2023, January 10). *4 kinds of brainstorming*. The Tech Edvocate. https://www.thetechedvocate.org/4-kinds-of-brainstorming/

Lyu, W., & Liu, J. (2021). Soft skills, hard skills: What matters most? Evidence from job postings. *Applied Energy, 300*, 117307.

MacLeod, C. (2016). *The social skills guidebook: Manage shyness, improve your conversations, and make friends, without giving up who you are.* Chris MacLeod.

Malala Yousafzai Quotes. (n.d.). BrainyQuote.com. Retrieved June 28, 2024, from BrainyQuote.com Web site: https://www.brainyquote.com/quotes/malala_yousafzai _662458

Marchi, A., Csajbók, Z., & Jonason, P. K. (2023). 24 ways to be compatible with your relationship partners: Sex differences, context effects, and love styles. *Personality and Individual Differences, 206,* 112134.

Margaret Thatcher Quotes. (n.d.). BrainyQuote.com. Retrieved June 25, 2024, from BrainyQuote.com Web site: https://www.brainyquote.com/quotes/margaret_thatche r_127095

Masterson, V. (2022, April 25). Which European countries have the most digital skills? *World Economic Forum.*

https://www.weforum.org/agenda/2022/04/europe-basic-digital-skills/

McKeown, M. (2012). *Adaptability: The art of winning in an age of uncertainty*. Kogan Page Publishers.

Meyer, J. (1990). Ronald Reagan and humor: A politician's velvet weapon. *Communication Studies, 41*(1), 76-88.

Miller, M. J., Woehr, D. J., & Hudspeth, N. (2002). The meaning and measurement of work ethic: Construction and initial validation of a multidimensional inventory. *Journal of Vocational Behavior, 60*(3), 451-489.

Miller, S. L. (2009). *Why teams win: 9 keys to success in business, sport and beyond*. John Wiley & Sons.

Morgenstern, J. (2004). *Time management from the inside out: the foolproof system for taking control of your schedule-- and your life*. Holt Paperbacks.

Murphy, S. (2015). *The optimistic workplace: Creating an environment that energizes everyone*. Hardcover.

National Foundation for Credit Counseling [NFCC]. (n.d.). https://www.nfcc.org

NerdWallet. (n.d.). https://www.nerdwallet.com

New King James Version. (1982). *Holy Bible*. Thomas Nelson. (Original work published 1982)

Newsweek. (1988, October 24). *Mr. Chips: Steve Jobs puts the 'wow' back in computers* [Magazine cover].

Nica, E., & Mirică, C. O. (2017). Are increasing student loan debt levels burdening graduates?. *Journal of Self-Governance and Management Economics, 5*(2), 68.

Notter, J., & Grant, M. (2012). *Humanize: How people-centric organizations succeed in a social world*. Que publishing.

O'Neal, S. (2012). *The duality of humor and aggression in leadership styles* (Doctoral dissertation, Barry University).

Ong, A. D., Burrow, A. L., & Fuller-Rowell, T. E. (2012). Positive emotions and the social broadening effects of Barack Obama. *Cultural Diversity and Ethnic Minority Psychology*, *18*(4), 424.

Overall, N. C., Sibley, C. G., & Travaglia, L. K. (2010). Loyal but ignored: The benefits and costs of constructive communication behavior. *Personal relationships*, *17*(1), 127-148.

Palmer, C. (2018). *Now what, grad?: Your path to success after college*. Rowman & Littlefield.

Pawar, R., Kulkarni, S., & Patil, S. (2020). Project based learning: An innovative approach for integrating 21st century skills. *Journal of Engineering Education Transformations*, *33*(4).

Pelekh, Y., & Shlikhta, G. (2024). 21st century skills and individual basic values of the future IT specialist: Education perspective. *The New Educational Review*, *75*, 176-188.

Pierce, D. (2015). A promising development. *Community College Journal, 86*(2), 22-25.

Pollak, L. (2019). *The remix: How to lead and succeed in the multigenerational workplace*. HarperCollins.

Porter, G. (2005). A "career" work ethic versus just a job. *Journal of European Industrial Training, 29*(4), 336-352.

Prike, T., Butler, L. H., & Ecker, U. K. (2024). Source-credibility information and social norms improve truth discernment and reduce engagement with misinformation online. *Scientific Reports, 14*(1), 6900.

Qualman, E. (2011). *Digital leader: 5 simple keys to success and influence*. McGraw Hill.

Qualman, E. (2012). *Socialnomics: How social media transforms the way we live and do business*. John Wiley & Sons.

Rainer Thom, S., & Rainer Jess, W. (2011). The millennials connecting to Americas largest generation.

Reiman, T. (2007). *The power of body language: How to succeed in every business and social encounter*. Simon and Schuster.

Ritchie, D. (2018, September 26). Building an agile, change-ready culture: Q&A with Studer Group President Debbie Ritchie. *Huron*. https://www.huronconsultinggroup.com/insights/building-an-agile-change-ready-culture

River, A. (2023). *Mindful communication: A guide to mastering conversations in the Workplace*. Kindle Edition

Roepe, L. R. (2017). Why soft skills will help you get the job and the promotion. *Revista Forbes*.

Schaffer, S. (2019, June 1). *A focus on the soft skills that healthcare executives need in order to be successful*. CSuite Solutions. https://csuitesolutions.com/healthcare-advisors/a-focus-on-the-soft-skills-that-healthcare-executives-need-in-order-to-be-successful/

Schawbel, D. (2018). *Back to human: How great leaders create connection in the age of isolation*. Hachette UK.

Schroth, H. (2019). Are you ready for Gen Z in the workplace? *California Management Review, 61*(3), 5-18.

Schwartz, J., Rogers, M., & Sandza, R. (1988, October 24). Steve Jobs comes back. *Newsweek, 112*(17), 46-51.

Schweinsberg, M., Thau, S., & Pillutla, M. M. (2022). Negotiation impasses: Types, causes, and resolutions. *Journal of Management, 48*(1), 49-76.

Shukla, S. (2016, September 24). *How lateral thinking is solving today's workplace design problems*. LinkedIn. https://www.linkedin.com/pulse/how-lateral-thinking-solving-todays-workplace-design-problems-shukla/

Steils, N., Martin, A., & Toti, J. F. (2022). Managing the transparency paradox of social-media influencer disclosures: How to improve authenticity and engagement when disclosing influencer–sponsor relationships. *Journal of Advertising Research, 62*(2), 148-166.

Stemmle, D. (2019). *Time management secrets for college students: The underground playbook for managing school, work, and fun.* [College Success].

Student Loan Hero [SLH]. (n.d.). https://studentloanhero.com

Taussig, D. (2021). *What we mean by the American Dream: Stories we tell about meritocracy.* ILR Press.

Taylor, R. M. (2016). Open-mindedness: An intellectual virtue in the pursuit of knowledge and understanding. *Educational theory, 66*(5), 599-618.

Torpey, E. (2019). *High-wage occupations by typical entry-level education, 2017. U.S. Bureau of Labor Statistics.*

https://www.bls.gov/careeroutlook/2019/article/high-wage-occupations.htm

Tracy, B. (2017). *Eat that frog!: 21 great ways to stop procrastinating and get more done in less time*. Berrett-Koehler Publishers.

Ward, D. E., Park, L. E., Walsh, C. M., Naragon-Gainey, K., Paravati, E., & Whillans, A. V. (2021). For the love of money: The role of financially contingent self-worth in romantic relationships. *Journal of Social and Personal Relationships, 38*(4), 1303-1328.

Wats, M., & Wats, R. K. (2009). Developing soft skills in students. *International Journal of Learning, 15*(12).

White, C. (2023). *Overcoming social anxiety step by step: A self-help action plan to conquer social anxiety, overcome shyness, and cultivate confidence*. Amazon.com Services LLC.

Wu, R. (2020). America's unforgiving forgiveness program:

    Problems and solutions for public service loan

    forgiveness. *Hastings LJ, 72,* 959.

Zauner, S., & Karp, M. (2020). Leveraging technology to increase

    student success. *Student Success in the Community*

    College: What Really Works?, 39.

Zebrowitz, L. A. (2004). The origin of first impressions. *Journal of*

    Cultural and Evolutionary Psychology, 2(1-2), 93-108.

Zhang, Y., & Benayoun, M. (2020). The emotional statement:

    profile photo and self-branding in the art world.

    International Journal of Arts and Technology, 12(2), 174-

    196.

ABOUT THE AUTHOR

Dr. Yaw Amponsah Adoo is a distinguished management professional with extensive experience in collegiate instruction, organizational leadership, and professional development. His work, spanning over a decade, focuses on employee motivation, well-being, and the effects of organizational change. Dr. Adoo's expertise includes job insecurity, work-related stressors, and workplace spirituality.

As Chair of the Department of Business at Morris Brown College, Dr. Adoo has also served in significant roles at Shorter University and The University of the Virgin Islands. In August 2024, he accepted an invitation to join the Harvard Business Review's Advisory Council, where he will provide valuable insights and shape content for management and leadership studies. His leadership extends beyond academia through partnerships promoting curriculum development and cultural appreciation.

www.ingramcontent.com/pod-product-compliance
Lightning Source LLC
Chambersburg PA
CBHW030906120626
46554CB00001B/19